Little Chicken Tales

Henry A. Buchanan

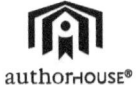

authorHOUSE®

AuthorHouse™
1663 Liberty Drive
Bloomington, IN 47403
www.authorhouse.com
Phone: 1-800-839-8640

First published by AuthorHouse 3/5/2010

ISBN: 978-1-4490-7959-8 (e)
ISBN: 978-1-4490-7958-1 (sc)

This book is printed on acid-free paper.

Contents

INTRODUCTION TO THE BOOK
OF LITTLE CHICKEN TALES

By Henry A. Buchanan

I brought the Little Chickens home with me because I needed something exciting in my life. That's not to say that Taffy and Max are not exciting. They are. In their own ways. But I wanted something more, and the Little Chickens were just made to fill that need.

But about Taffy and Max. Because these two were with me before the Little Chickens. Taffy is a little white Eskimo Spitz, and you will read more about her when we get into the chicken tales. She has been my constant companion for many years, and her loyalty to me is unquestioned. But I was not thinking of Taffy when I got the chickens, even though she was there with me, looking on with her bright black eyes full of excitement, her pointed ears standing up at attention.

Max, the Manx Cat, is capable of creating excitement too. And I have told you about Max in the little book TALE OF THE CAT WHO HAD NO TAIL. But just in case you have not read that tale, I will tell you now that Max is a big yellow cat, although he was just a little yellow kitten when he came into my life by way of the big oak tree where

I found him pacing back and forth on a limb that overhung the lawn. He didn't have a tail then and he doesn't have a tail now because Manx Cats don't have tails. He does not miss what he never had though, and he is a complete cat without a tail, which may seem strange to cats who do have tails.

Two gold fishes live in the aquarium, but gold fishes don't make life exciting. They make a lot of work for people who put them in fish tanks, but you never hear a peep out of gold fishes; they just swim and stare at you silently.

There are birds too, mostly birds of passage, so they don't figure prominently in this story. They just share the scratch feed and shelled corn that I put out for the Little Chickens to eat. So, back to the Little Chickens. Bantams. Or Banties they are called. They were not what I got first when I went to Trade Day at Mayfield.

First was the Big Red Rooster, and of course I had to have two hens with him. They were speckled grey hens and since I had nothing to trade for them, I just bought them, paying out greenbacks which immediately sends the signal that the buyer is not a trader. But I bought those three and took them home in cardboard boxes with slits cut in them for air, and I put them in the chicken house which has a chicken pen attached, and I waited for those fresh eggs which are better than anything I could buy at the grocery store.

The Big Red Rooster became known as Big Red, and the two speckled grey hens were Grey Hen Number One and Grey Hen Number Two, but I really could not tell them apart. Big Red mated with both of them and didn't seem to show any preference so I dismissed all concern about that little matter. I went back to Trade Day and this time I came home with two guineas. I was told that one of them was a hen and the other a cock, and I was told how to distinguish them, but to tell the truth, they looked alike to me, and they made a lot of noise and they were a source of interest and curiosity because people asked me what I wanted with them and I wondered about it myself.

So I went back to Trade Day at Mayfield the next Saturday and got my first pair of Banties. I didn't have any trouble about which was male and female. Anybody with eyes and ears can tell the difference. Bantie roosters have high combs and long curving tail feathers. And they crow often and loud. The hens are smaller and quieter and not so flashy. So now I was in the Little Chicken business, and the Little Bantie Rooster immediately became known as Little Red, as opposed to Big Red, who saw him as the enemy, and Big Red trounced Little Red so harshly that I saw I had to do something about the imbalance. I took Big Red back to Trade Day and traded him for a new pair of Banties. The new ones were golden in color, and Little Red quickly proved to Golden Boy that in the absence of Big Red, he was now the Cock of the Roost. Then I became unhappy about those guineas who were making a great deal of noise, beating up on the Banties, and not laying any eggs.

I took the guineas to Trade Day – I had now become recognized as a trader and I traded them for another pair of Banties. These new birds were Grey, so the rooster became known as Grey Boy and his mate was Little Grey Hen. I was in the Bantie business. It was exciting.

Soon I was getting all the eggs I could eat. Big eggs and little eggs. The Big Grey Hens, Numbers One and Two, were laying the big eggs, and the Little Bantie Hens were laying the little eggs. At some point in this rapid development of my flock, I bought a couple more pairs – the man would not sell hens without the roosters – and my little flock had grown to about a dozen chickens, but Little Red had maintained the place of Supreme Ruler, for each time a new cock was introduced, Little Red let him know who was the Boss Cock, and Little Red held this Top Spot until a conspiracy took place, and life in the chicken yard began to look a lot like international politics which I have to tell you about.

At this time the President of the United States began to say that there must be a Regime Change in Iraq where Saddam Hussein was President, or put in the language of the hen house, Cock of the Flock in Iraq. And to tell you about what happened next, I have to create a fictional character to take place in the life of the flock of Little Chickens because a story like this just seems to need a fictional character, and here he is: Barney.

Now I will not try to tell you that Barney is not myself in fictional form. Indeed, you may see me hiding behind the character of Barney if you look closely enough. But if I represent myself in the first person singular, doing all the strange things and saying all the strange things that Barney does, you may begin to think that I have been living alone too long because Barney and Taffy and Max and the Little Chickens all seem to be on such an even keel in the matter of communications, that it may seem to you that this Little Book of Little Chicken Tales is really about some people you know.

TALE ONE: REGIME CHANGE
IN THE HEN HOUSE

Barney stood open mouthed, gazing at the red blaze in the Eastern Sky. It spread across the horizon, heralding a brisk, cool October day. The fiery blaze rose, spreading, mixing at last with the blue above. The glory began to fade. All was silence around him. Then the first cock crowed, followed by another, then another, and yet another. Shrill, high pitched, hoarse, strangled. The little Bantam cocks were greeting the dawn. They came down from their roost pole in the old barn. The little hens followed. Cocks crowed. Hens sang. Barney listened for a familiar but absent voice. "Where is Little Red?"

The little red banty rooster had disappeared without leaving a feather of evidence. "I'll bet that chicken hawk got Little Red." Barney's concern deepened as he thought about the hawk he had seen sailing over the bean field, his all seeing eyes searching, his moving shadow sending the flock of banties scurrying for cover under the Forsythia bush. But Little Red was cocky to the edge of folly. Had he challenged the hawk? Tried to fight him off the flock? He wouldn't have the ghost of a chance against the talons and beak of the hawk.

Barney faced the sunrise, thinking: This is a one time spectacle. The sun rose yesterday; it will rise tomorrow. But this is today. Unlike any other day. The cocks are greeting it. Four of them. A chorus of songs. Each different. The little hens were singing too. But no Little Red. Barney searched among the flock for the familiar figure of Little Red. "Little Red's gone."

The little roosters threw their heads back. They threw their chests out. Their necks stretched, then inflated. Ruffs of feathers on their necks rose as they called, challenging. Then silence. Followed by a sound. Barney heard a cock's crow behind him and at a distance of fifty yards. Could it be an echo? The interval was too long for an echo. Then could it be Little Red? But where? The cocks in the hen yard crowed again. A veritable cacophony of cock crowing. After a long interval, a muffled reply. He turned toward the sound. Still asking Is it Little Red? Or an echo of the birds here at my feet?

Barney turned away from the blazing sky and from the singing in the hen yard. He walked back to the garage. At the closed doors of the garage darkness still prevailed. He threw open the doors, peered in. From a darkened corner a cock's crow sounded. Shrill, strangled, but brave. He focused on that darkened corner, drew nearer, and gradually a form, huddled in darkness, became visible. Then a reptilian head raised out of the huddled dark feathers. Little Red crowed.

What had happened in Barney's hen yard? Little Red had been Cock of the Roost, and now he had taken refuge on the shelf among the oil cans and cardboard boxes and gardening tools.

Yes, he was answering the challenging calls of the cocks in the hen yard. But from a distance. And from his hiding place in the darkened garage. Hardly the place to greet the rising sun.

Barney caught Little Red up in his hands and stroked him reassuringly. Speaking softly to the little rooster, he returned him to the hen yard. But immediately, the cocks there attacked. They pounced on the fallen leader and began pecking him, driving him unmercifully into a corner of the fence. All except Little Grey Boy. Golden Boy and the three Reds, all clad in iridescent plumage, ran at Little Red and beat him with wings, beaks and feet. Little Red crouched in the fence corner; his eyes were wild with fear; he searched desperately for escape. Barney came to the rescue. But Oh how the mighty had fallen! How could this be?

Little Red, with his mate Little Brown Hen, had been Barney's first purchase at Trade Day in Mayfield. Among all the chickens and ducks and pea fowls and rabbits and even baby goats on display in their cages, Little Red, crowing boldly in his wire pen, had caught Barney's eye. He was small but cocky. His red comb had been trimmed for fighting. His spurs were sharp like briars. His chest stood out like a pouter pigeon. His tail feathers curved like a scythe. When the sunlight struck him the black and red iridescence was a glory to behold.

Barney took Little Red and Little Brown Hen home and for a week Little Red strutted about the hen house; it was his throne room, and when, a week later, a new pair of Greys came, Little Red quickly defeated Grey Boy and remained the King. Each week for a month Barney brought a new pair. The Goldens. The Three Reds. And each time Little Red whipped the newcomer. But now Little Red had been whipped by a coalition of the four Golden Red cocks. Only Little Grey Boy remained neutral.

But how had the four cocks reached the decision to break the tyranny of Little Red? With what language and with what barnyard psychology had they overthrown him? What had happened? The mystery remains, but Little Red now runs free over the lawn; he seeks cover under the privet bush and the Forsythia and when the flock is turned out on the lawn he runs with the hens and with Little Grey Boy, but he keeps his distance from the four cocks who overthrew him. At dusk when the flock returns to the roost pole in the hen house, Little Red goes to his shelf in the garage. He settles among the oil cans and cardboard boxes and gardening tools.

At dawn, when the cacophony of cock calls rises from the hen house Little Red answers the Alliance of Four with his own high, shrill, strangled call. But Golden Boy is now the King of the Roost, with his able Red Lieutenants.

Tale Two: A Mate For Little Red

"**P**oor little fellow." Barney studied Little Red who was making strident sounds of alarm. "Scared. Yes, he's scared. But he's lonesome. There's the real trouble. That little rooster is lonesome."

The attentive reader will remember that Little Red, once the proud Cock of the Roost, had been dethroned and driven out of the henyard by a coalition of Red and Golden cocks. They now kept him at bay. If he dared to approach the flock when hens and roosters together were running over the lawn, they would move threateningly and send him fleeing away in disgrace. Little Red stirred something inside Barney. A visceral response. "I have to do something about Little Red or he will die of the lonelies."

Barney, himself, lived alone ...except for Taffy the little white dog and Max the yellow Manx cat and the chickens and the fish in the aquarium. And of course the birds at the feeders in the back yard. Still, without anyone of the same species, a condition which Scripture says caused God to make woman as the crown of creation. "Yes," Barney said, "I have to get a mate for Little Red. A little hen to keep him company."

So Barney went back to Trade Day at Mayfield. There he found a whole cage full of chickens, little grey chickens and little golden chickens and little brown and speckled chickens. Only one among all these little chickens caught and held Barney's eye.

He could not say exactly what color the little hen was. A lavender, or beige, or grey, all blended into softness with a few speckles on her breast. Different from all the others. "This is the one," he said to the bearded old man in overalls. "She's for Little Red." And the old man remembered Little Red. "I told you they'd fight if you put all them roosters in there together," he had said. Now he smiled through a yellow, tobacco stained beard, and he caught the little hen whose color Barney could not define. Together Barney and the old man gently fitted the little hen into the cardboard box and Barney cut little slits in the box with the bone handled pocket knife that would hardly cut hot butter, and he set the box on the back seat of his car and drove home. "Now I'll just wait for evening and then I will introduce them."

All day long the little hen crouched quietly in the cardboard box with the slits for ventilation. Barney slipped some scratch feed and a little jar of water inside the box and spoke softly to her. Then he went inside the house to wait for evening. He picked up H.G. Wells' story about the Martians, and he weighed it against Shakespeare's Julius Caesar. Unable to decide which to read, he took turns reading a chapter from the Martians and an Act from Shakespeare. With this frightening regimen of reading, he almost forgot about the little hen in the box, but it was a cloudy day in November, and when he noticed that evening was coming on fast he went out to the garage to check on the cardboard box with the little hen inside it. Taffy reared up on the door to let him know that she was going too, and Max made a dash for it when he opened the door, then went humping along with his back bowed up and glancing sideways because he liked to frighten the chickens and watch them go into hysterics. Taffy hadn't much interest in the chickens, but she liked to get in their house to see what they were eating, and this sent them flying into all the corners of the house and pen.

The little hen in the box was quiet. Barney said "Stand back Taffy. You too Max." And he slipped the little hen gently from the box and held her close to him for a moment. Then he set her on the roof of the old car. He had not noticed that Little Red was already in the garage, but when he set the hen up there Little Red cackled as if he had just made a big discovery, and he seemed to be about to run out of the garage, but he didn't, and Barney said "Now we will see what you will do about this."

Little Red set up such a crowing that anybody who had been taking an afternoon nap would wake up and think it was daybreak instead of sunset. Barney went back to his reading but he couldn't concentrate, and in a few minutes he slipped out and peeped through the garage window. Little Red and the little hen were together on the ground; they were becoming acquainted. Tentatively. The little hen seemed a bit shy, and Little Red, filled with wonder, was standing taller than usual. Barney was filled with wonder too; he wondered what they would do next. "I wonder," he said, "if they will roost together." But when darkness came on he took the flashlight, threw the beam onto the roof of the old car and saw Little Red crouched in his customary position there but the little hen was not with him.

Barney went back toward the house, calling to Max who bounded out of nowhere and dashed in through the door ahead of him. Taffy took up her position for watching on the old rug that served for a footpad on the front porch. Taffy is a watchdog and she takes her duty seriously.

He had decided to stick with H.G. Wells and the Martians until he could get a clear idea of what a Martian is, but he was getting hungry too, so Barney put some apples in the oven to bake, thinking he could read without having to worry about something boiling over or burning on top of the stove. In fact, he was still thinking about Little Red and the little hen of uncertain color, and he said to Max who had now got on his lap and stretched out with his head hanging over Barney's knee. "She won't sleep with him tonight but we will see what happens in the morning."

The moon was full. Barney could not sleep, and at three in the morning he left his bed and turned on the coffee pot, only to discover that the apples in the oven had been cooking all night and were very well done, so when the coffee stopped burbling he had an apple with his first cup of coffee. This time he went back to Shakespeare's Julius Caesar and waited impatiently for daylight.

Little Red was not fooled by the moonlight. He was waiting for daylight, and when the dawn did come it was heralded by a cacophony of cock crows from the hen yard. Little Red responded to their challenge with a boldness that had been missing from his morning song since he was driven out by the Alliance of Red and Golden cocks.

Max had stretched himself on the table among Barney's books, and Taffy was waiting to be called before she would arise. Barney slipped out to check on Little Red and the little hen but both Taffy and Max beat him to the door and ran out ahead of him. At the garage Barney turned on the light. Little Red was still crouched on the roof of the old car, but although he searched in every dark corner and looked among the boxes, buckets and tools on all the shelves, Barney could not find the little hen.

"Now won't it be the pits if some varmint has sneaked in here and got her while she was sleeping?" Barney shooed Little Red off the roof of the old car, backed it out onto the driveway, and looked in all the dark corners again. NO

LITTLE HEN. But no feathers on the ground either. "Thank the Lord for that." Barney found some solace there.

Barney went back inside to have a third cup of coffee. He was both disconsolate and hopeful. Disconsolate because the little hen had disappeared, and hopeful because there was no evidence of foul play in the form of feathers scattered about. "Going to have to make this place varmint proof though," he decided out loud for Taffy to hear.

After his third cup of coffee Barney went outside again. This time he found Little Red in the narrow space between the hen house and the Forsythia bush, but he did not see the little hen. Still, there was something about Little Red that rang a bell; he was different now. Standing tall. Cocky. "Feeling his oats," Barney said. Then he called "Chick Chick. Here Chick Chick." He sprinkled a little scratch feed on the ground at the edge of the Forsythia bush. Little Hen came running from under the Forsythia bush. She was as bright eyed as a new bride and she started scratching about as busily as a little housewife.

Little Red scratched his wing with his foot, threw his head back, pushed out his chest like a pouter pigeon, flapped his wings and crowed lustily.

A footnote to this romantic episode in the life of Little Red: On the second evening of their marriage Little Hen did not return with Little Red to the safety of the roof of the old car in the garage. No. She perched high on an upper branch of the Forsythia bush near the hen house. Barney feared she might fall prey to a night prowling predator but when morning came, cloudy, foggy, misty, threatening snow, with no visible sunrise, Little Hen sat still in the Forsythia bush and Little Red was seen running eagerly, excited by the prospect of reunion toward the Forsythia bush where Little Hen waited.

TALE THREE: LITTLE RED
BATTLES AGAIN

"Come on out." Barney flung the door open and called to the flock of hens and cocks standing with upraised heads and expectant eyes in the chicken house. "It's Christmas. Celebrate."

It was, in fact, three days after Christmas. But there are twelve days of Christmas and some laying hens on one of them. On this third day of Christmas the sun was shining brightly, the air was brisk and invigorating. It was just a good day for being outside. "So come on," he called to them, and winked at Taffy who was standing nearby and watching the parade as the hens and roosters came running. Ah. The joy of freedom. Outside, they clucked and talked among themselves about the wonderful things they were finding under the Forsythia bush. The cocks flapped their wings, strutted, crowed loudly, and even made suggestive passes at the hens. The hens, not taking them seriously, went about the business of scratching and pecking for bits of food invisible to Barney.

Taffy yipped, threatened to dash into the flock and scatter them, but at a signal from Barney, settled for watching them. Her attention was diverted by a neighbor's strange dog who trotted through the yard, sending the chickens all flying into the tree limbs and onto the roofs of hen house and tool shed. Taffy they knew, but this fellow looked like a cross between a fox and a jackal and they were not trusting him. So they all crouched on their high perches and looked down anxiously until Taffy had driven the strange dog away into the bean field. When he had gone slinking home the hens and cocks began to come down again to the ground. But they were still nervous. Barney counted them as they came down. All eight of them were on the ground. But what about Little Red, Golden Boy and their shared mate, Little Hen. And something strange had occurred in the midst of the turmoil caused by the strange dog. Instead of eight chickens, he now counted nine. A closer look told him that Number Nine was Little Red, who had come out of the garage and was facing the Red and Golden Cocks who had driven him into exile.

First, one of the larger Red and Golden cocks approached Little Red and was driven off, but he was immediately replaced by another who seemed more eager for the fray. Little Red attacked this second challenger and the battle was on. Barney stood aside to watch. "Keep an eye open for that dog, Taffy," he said. "We don't want any interference. This may be the fight that will determine the course of events in the hen yard for the future."

Barney's friend Joe had come to visit and talk with Barney. Now he was engrossed in watching the developing struggle for power and control among the cocks. "This is Little Red's chance to win back the throne," Joe said. "And it looks like he just might do it."

The two cocks fought, flying up against each other, reaching for the head with a vicious beak, drawing their spurs across the exposed chest. The ruff on Little Red's neck rose and stood out like an English dandy of two or three centuries ago. He leaped onto the larger cock and gave him a vicious peck on the head. The Red and Gold and Blue cock went down, his eyes blinked and he seemed to be about to give up the fight.

"I believe Little Red is going to be the cock of the roost again," Barney said to his friend Joe who had come to watch the fight. Taffy barked excitedly and glanced at Barney. She was saying "Just let me get in there and I will determine who is winner of this fracas. And it won't be either of those two."

Max came and watched too. He was afraid to interfere because he had once been flogged by the big hens and he was not willing to risk it again.

Both cocks were becoming tired now, and each successive attack was slower and less forceful. Then the larger cock landed on Little Red's back and pecked at his comb. His extra size and weight was wearing Little Red down. But Little Red came out and struck a hard blow on his adversary. The battle warmed up again, but soon it slowed again. The battling cocks were striking with beak and talon. Rising, ducking, each seeking to escape the worst blows. Then Little Red weakened, lowered his head, turned and tried to escape.

The larger cock followed him, gathering strength from the victory. Little Red turned the corner of the garage, and the other cock gave up the chase and turned back toward the flock under the Forsythia bush.

Little Red rejoined Grey Boy and Little Hen in the garage. They received him gladly. He was still their hero. Barney looked for blood and sign of torn feathers. "A good fight. Little Red." Barney spoke with pride. "You fought bravely. And one of these days ... Who knows?"

A flurry of cackling and flapping of wings in the hen house called Barney back to that area. A Big Grey Hen was leaving the nest. Barney put his hand into the nest and found a warm egg. He turned to his friend Joe. "While the cocks fight, the hens go about their business ... Well, here's half my breakfast."

Tale Four: A Threat From Down Under

After that first meeting of Little Red and Little Hen the romance was a daytime thing with lonesome nights. Little Red came early each evening to his place on the roof of the old car. But Little Hen perched on a high branch of the forsythia bush. Barney said to Taffy who was ready to bark at Little Hen in the bush "This is no way for a marriage to go anyplace. Besides, if some night prowling varmint comes he could climb right up there and pluck her off that branch like a ripe plum."

He studied her, thinking he might be able to catch her and take her inside the garage but she looked back at him with round scared eyes. He thought she might escape him and hide somewhere on the ground and become easy prey, and he turned away to the garage where he attempted to get the lawn mower out and see if it would start. His first attempt failed. The lawn mower would not roll and when he jerked it he found that it was sitting on a mound of fresh dirt. When he had dragged the mower off the mound he made another surprising discovery. A hole in the ground only a few inches from the edge of the mound of dirt. The hole was about three inches in diameter and he peered into the dark burrow but could see nothing. Taffy came and nudged Barney aside. She poked her muzzle into the hole and snorted, then withdrew with dirt on her nose. She looked up at Barney, her eyes asking if he wanted her to dig into this mystery, but before Barney could make up his mind, Taffy decided against it. Judging from the size of the pile of dirt, the burrow must run to China, or at least to the edge of the bean field.

Barney and Taffy both studied the dark hole in the ground and Barney said "Now we have a problem. If I leave Little Hen in the bush some prowler may climb up there and get her. If I bring her in here whatever is in this hole may come out and catch her. I was planning on making the garage varmint proof so nothing could get in and now it's already in here, or down there somewhere in the hole in the ground.

Taffy yipped impatiently and this triggered something in Barney's brain. "A trap," he said. "I'll get a trap and catch the little devil whatever he is." Barney drove to the farm store, with Taffy sitting up beside him, and when they got there the man said he had traps but he did not know how they work. "I just work here," he said. "I am not a trapper." He showed Barney a steel trap with jaws and a little platform for the bait and a metal piece to spring the trigger. Barney tried to open the trap. It was strong. Finally he pressed it open with his boot and Taffy came to investigate the thing. "Stay back Taffy" Barney said. "If you get your nose in the jaws of this trap it will be Katie Bar the Door for you." He raised his foot and the jaws snapped together viciously.

Back home again, Barney baited the trap with a piece of bacon, pressed down with his boot until the jaws were open, and set the trigger, warning Taffy again to stay clear. He drove a nail in the wall to hook the chain, set the trap beside the pile of fresh dirt, and went inside to contemplate the dangers that confront a trapper. Max made a terrible racket in the utility room and came into the kitchen with a small mouse dangling from his mouth. He set the mouse down on the floor and it ran and hid behind Taffy's food bowl.

That same evening Barney found Little Hen on her chosen perch in the Forsythia bush, while Little Red crouched on the roof of the old car. But he was confident that his trap would get the varmint who was planning to eat Little Hen, so he waited until dark, and flashlight in hand, he lifted Little Hen off her perch in the Forsythia bush and carried her, unprotesting, to the garage. There he set her gently down beside Little Red and slipped away with a backward glance at the trap beside the varmint's hole.

With the life of Little Hen and the happiness of Little Red at stake Barney did not rest well that night. To fight off anxiety he immersed himself in Shakespeare's Tempest and H.G. Wells' story of the Martian invasion of earth. At last his eyelids were droopy; he fell asleep and awakened an hour before dawn, resisted the temptation to go too early to check his trap, and drank coffee until daylight began to seep in through the window.

Inside the garage he found Little Red and Little Hen still sitting on the roof of the old car. Then he threw the beam of the flashlight into the dark corner where he had set the trap. But there was no trap. A closer look revealed the chain still fastened to the wall but where was the trap? He took hold on the chain and pulled. Out came the trap from under a pile of fresh dirt.

"Now this is strange," Barney said to Taffy who had followed him and was watching eagerly to see what was in the trap. "Stand back, old girl. The trap's not been sprung; it could get you if you poke your nose in it. But look, the bacon's gone. What's going on here?"

Back inside the house, Barney poured another cup of coffee. He was on the point of commenting on the present state of affairs to Max. Then he noticed that Max had surprised a tiny mouse near the big bag of chicken feed and he was playing Cat and Mouse with his prey who was not enjoying the game as much as Max was. The game was much more interesting to Max than the mystery of the underground varmint that was threatening the health and happiness of Little Red and Little Hen.

The third day of the marriage of the two little Banties dawned damp, chilly and cloudy. Barney, a creature of habit himself, went off to the Sunrise Cafe to drink more coffee and puzzle over the strange underground threat which had foiled his first attempt to entrap him. Little Red and his quiet little mate, unaware of, or unconcerned about, the underground creature who had come to dominate Barney's mind, remained in the garage, happily pecking at the scratch feed in the plastic pan. Barney sat over his coffee cup at the Sunrise. "I will try again tonight," he vowed. The girl who stood nearby with a coffee pot in hand, looked at him with question marks in her eyes. He nodded toward the coffee pot and said "Then we will see what we will see."

Evening came, and Barney baited the trap with a pat of butter and a dollop of cat food while Max looked on, suspecting him of larceny or worse. He reset the trap, cautioning the little chickens who were still getting acquainted and seemed to have forgotten the larger flock in the hen house. "Now don't get into the trap." As an added precaution he stretched chicken wire over his whole trapping endeavor.

He went back inside the house and found Max lying in his chair. He carefully lifted him, sat down and set Max on his lap, but Max was not happy with this arrangement; he climbed onto the table and lay down beside Shakespeare's Tempest and began licking himself.

The afternoon dragged by on leaden feet while Barney waited for the evening and another attempt to trap the varmint. Taffy did her best to make life exciting for him. She saw the neighbor's old black dog chasing a small herd of deer across the wheat field and she barked wildly, either at the deer who ran in an easy manner as if the dog posed no real threat, or at the dog, or at both the deer and the dog. She glanced back at Barney as if to say "Now here is something worth looking at and all on top of the ground too."

Max had found his tiny mouse again and was tormenting him with no conscience of wrong doing. When evening finally came Barney slipped into the garage. Little Red was crouched on the roof of the old car. Little Hen had reached the deck lid and seemed satisfied with this intermediate height. Barney said "Good. I may not catch the varmint. But he won't catch them tonight." With this neutral state of affairs he returned to Shakespeare's Tempest and to Wells' Martians. The narrator of this tale is well aware that the reader may be wondering when it will come to some defining conclusion, but all the story teller can say is "Not Yet." And so we must await a new day and whatever revelations that new dawn may bring.

The new day dawned but it brought no new revelation. Little Red and Little Hen were still there and the trap was still there; more fresh dirt was piled on top of the trap, and Barney remained perplexed but determined to get to the bottom of the mystery. So he passed the day in wondering and the evening came and he checked on Little Red and Little Hen again at the edge of darkness, but when he threw the beam of light onto the old car the little chickens were missing. "Something is wrong here," he muttered, ignoring the evident concern in Taffy's eyes. "Have they gone back to the Forsythia bush?"

A close inspection of the Forsythia bush, conducted with flashlight beam searching the branches and the ground underneath, convinced him that they had not gone back to the Forsythia bush. The leaves were falling off following the first heavy frost, but no roosting chickens were to be found among those leaves and branches. He went back to the garage and searched in all the dark corners but, he saw no chickens.

He continued the search into the adjoining tool shed but he could not see Little Red and Little Hen. Then he heard a soft, quiet whistling, almost inaudible, but it caught his attention, arrested him. Listening intently, he followed the faint sound, casting his flashlight beam into the shelves and tools scattered all about. Then Little Red's bright color was reflected in the light. Both of them had nestled among the tools on the highest shelf.

Breathing a sigh of relief, he checked the trap again and went back into the house. Max hopped onto his lap, stretched his long body, extended his arms, spread his paws, and unsheathed his claws. He pricked Barney's knee and yawned widely. "Easy there Boy." Barney picked up Shakespeare and the night passed as all the preceding nights of this episode had passed. Morning came, as the morning had been coming the whole week long. But on this morning when Barney went at first dawn to the still darkened garage, he did not need the light to reveal what he had caught in his trap. The nose knows some things, and Barney's nose told him what it knew. He had caught a skunk.

The jaws of the trap had done their cruel work on the invader from down under, but not before he had fired his weapon of defense. Pinching his nostrils together, Barney stared at the little black furred body with the white stripes running down its sides and he turned to Taffy. "Stand back

Girl. This is a serious business here. We may need that whole wheelbarrow load of fresh dirt to cover this."

Little Red and Little Hen were making sounds somewhere between wonder and alarm, but they did not seem inclined to desert this safe place. Better the skunk's odor than a renewed attack by the coalition of Red and Golden Cocks. Little Red threw his head back, he flapped his wings, he stretched his neck, he pushed his chest out like a pouter pigeon, and he crowed, loud and clear, and the Reds and the Goldens answered him from the hen yard, their voices mingling and competing with one another. Little Red crowed again and scratched his wing and Little Hen appeared both docile and proud.

Tale Five: One Hen...
How Many Nests?

The Little Grey Hen is practising to lay an egg. Each day she sits on one of her nests, and waits for an egg to emerge.

"One of her nests?" Taffy's eyes are two question marks. "How many nests does a hen need to lay an egg?"

"Well, now, she has three nests that I know about. There is the nest in the cardboard box here on the shelf among my tools. To be truthful, there are cans of nails and screws and pruners and a sickle and hammer and a saw and a few other things. But I put wheat straw in this little box to make it attractive and comfortable for her. And she likes it, for you see that she sits there for an hour each day. You can see her fiery red comb showing above the rim of the box. So she's trying."

"Well, and what happens?"

"Then she hops off the nest and drops to the floor and when I go and look inside the box, there is no egg."

"All that sitting on the nest, and no egg? Maybe she needs help."

"There is Little Red Rooster, her husband. He's the one who got caught by Ol' Blackie and carried off, but we got him back. Now he stands on top of the old piano. Waiting. Watching. Helping? Yes. Maybe it helps to have someone with you when you are trying to lay an egg. And she really does need help. No doubt about that."

"Yes, but isn't that little rooster inexperienced in the art of laying eggs? How can he help?"

"Indeed. But he seems to know what it is that she is trying to do and he wants to help."

"So maybe it's the cardboard box, and it isn't working."

"Could be. I suppose. But on other days the Little Grey Hen goes inside that big metal box on the shelf where I keep the gasoline and oil and things for the lawn mower."

"What things?"

"Well, there are the rat traps and other junk. But she goes in there and sits in the grass clippings, and it's dark and when she comes out, I reach in there, thinking what if there's a snake or a rat? But no egg, so my hand always comes back empty."

"And the Little Red Rooster?"

"Well, he stands among the oil cans and rat traps – they've been sprung of course – and sometimes he will crow just to let the other cocks in the hen yard know he's on duty. But it doesn't produce an egg."

"That doesn't work either then."

"No. But there is another nest. In the wheelbarrow."

"Wheelbarrow? That seems like a strange place for a hen nest."

"Well, I raked up the grass clippings after I mowed the lawn, and I piled them in the wheelbarrow because they had to be somewhere."

The Little Grey Hen has formed a perfectly round depression in the grass clippings. This little nest is just the right size for her diminutive body. And there she sits, patiently waiting for the egg which will herald the arrival of the next generation of Little Grey Hens and Little Red Roosters. But the egg never comes. Why? And when will the egg come? Barney waits too, with the Little Red Rooster.

Barney can't sit on the wheelbarrow handle the way the Little Red Rooster does. He can't sit among the oil cans and rat traps. He can't even sit on top of the old piano. He sits on a cushion on the front porch, with a yellow pad on his lap, pen in hand, waiting. For Barney is waiting to see what will happen in that little flock of little chickens because he thinks they may be trying to tell him something. Maybe something about life in the barnyard, and life in the nation and in the world, because the people who make up Barney's world are a lot like the little chickens.

"All this fighting for control of the hen yard. And all this obsession with laying an egg." Barney looks at Taffy, and wonders out loud. "What do you suppose these little chickens are trying to tell me about the world I am living in?"

Taffy looks back at Barney, and her eyes say "You are the doctor. I reckon you will have to figure it all out for yourself ... And when you get it all, let me know. Chickens and people. A big mystery. Why can't they be sensible? Like dogs."

TALE SIX: MYSTERY OF THE FIRST EGG

The quintessential question is not Which came first, the chicken or the egg? But Who laid that first egg? And that question had Barney, to say nothing of Taffy and Max, to say nothing even of the members of the little flock of Banties, wondering about the egg. But maybe the little Banties all knew. They were just keeping their secrets from Barney. Or else they were speaking and Barney could not understand what they were saying.

In any case, Little Grey Hen was the Prime Suspect. Little Grey Hen had been trying for two weeks to lay an egg. About mid morning she would hop up onto the shelf where Barney's tools were scattered in confusion which baffled even Barney when he wanted a screwdriver or the hammer. From the shelf she would hop into the cardboard box which stood on the shelf. Inside the cardboard box Barney had put wheat straw, and Little Grey Hen had twisted herself around in the wheat straw until she had formed a perfectly round nest. The nest was such a perfect nest for Little Grey Hen that she would sit there for hours, waiting. What was she waiting for? The egg, of course. Her red comb showed above the rim of the cardboard box, her bright eyes shone above the box top. Little Grey Hen was not taking a nap; she was waiting for the egg.

Little Grey Hen was not waiting alone. Little Red Rooster was waiting with her. Like a proud but anxious father in the waiting room of the Maternity Ward in the hospital, Little Red Rooster stood on top of the old piano. He was alert, watchful, waiting ... for the egg. Neither hunger nor thirst, nor sunshine nor rain, nor cool breezes nor suffocating heat, could induce Little Red Rooster to abandon his watchtower on the old piano. His eyes were fixed on Little Grey Hen. He was waiting.

But you, dear patient Reader, will now say to me What are Little Grey Hen and Little Red Rooster really waiting for? Is it nothing more than an egg like the egg I had for my breakfast this morning? It is indeed an egg, but it is much more than a mere egg that they are waiting for. They await the Miracle of Creation. The Dawning of a New Day. A New and Wonderful Dawning Day. The Herald of the Future. The Egg.

Little Grey Hen sat on the straw nest in the cardboard box for two and a half hours. Little Red Rooster stood on the old piano for that whole time. But when Little Grey Hen hopped down from the nest and went singing about on the floor, and when Little Red Rooster flew down from his watchtower on the old piano and went strutting over to Little Grey Hen, and scratching his wing feathers to say only God and little chickens know what to her. Then Barney slipped into the tool shed and peeped over into the cardboard box with its nest of straw, and there was no egg.

The two principal actors in this drama went happily to the front yard where they picked at invisible objects in the grass and they sang, that is Little Grey Hen sang, and Little Red Rooster crowed, which I suppose is a rooster's way of singing. And the two of them were perfectly happy with their morning's work of waiting. Only Barney was frustrated. Only Barney said "But there is no egg. Look here

Taffy. Look here Max. These two have spent the morning waiting and watching for the egg to come, and there is no egg here. What does it mean?" Barney said "I wonder if God ever got impatient about the Creation of the World." Did God ever say "When will that egg appear?"

Yes, Barney wondered about God and about Man, and now he wondered about little chickens, and he wondered if the little chickens would reveal something to him that would be helpful in his wondering about God and Man. So, when after days and days of watching Little Grey Hen sit on that nest in the cardboard box and watching Little Red Rooster standing guard on the old piano, one day Barney looked and saw an egg in the nest, he said "Eureka." Whatever Eureka means, it will be evident that it means Barney has made an important discovery because now he saw an egg in the nest. But no sooner than he saw the egg than he asked "But who laid that egg?" For he called both Taffy and Max to behold this wonder, but still he wondered because there was another little hen. She of the multiple names. First Hopeful. Then Hopeless. Then Hope Reborn.

You will have a proper introduction to her later. But now let us watch HHH. This little Triple hen is free again. She no longer sits on that nest in the black plastic bucket in the hen house, waiting for the one unhatched egg to hatch. She has abandoned that hopeless egg, and she is running with the cocks in the yard under the big maple tree with the wonderful bark artwork, and she is clucking and picking. Her comb is red, and her feathers are smooth and her movements are quick and lively. The cocks strut around her and they scratch their wings and threaten to mount her. And is it just possible that she has slipped into that nest of straw in the cardboard box and done in one day what Little Grey Hen has been trying for more than two weeks to do, without success?

Is it possible that there is a hidden mystery in this Miracle of Creation? Even a Trick? Does God sometimes play tricks on Man, just to keep him on his toes and remembering that he is Man and not God? And can it be that HHH has tricked both Little Grey Hen and Little Red Rooster, and even Barney, by slipping into that nest and laying an egg?

Barney said to Taffy "I have seen HHH running about the garage and the tool shed. Did she slip in there and lay that egg? Has she got ahead of Little Grey Hen who sits on the nest for two hours every day? There is only one way to find out."

Taffy had not been helpful at all. What she did propose to do was send the whole flock of little chickens flying into the trees. Max was less than helpful. He simply crouched low to the ground, waiting for the chickens to come back down.

So on the next day Barney fastened HHH, that's Hopeful, Hopeless, Hope Reborn, in the chicken house and he left Little Grey Hen running free in the yard. Little Grey Hen got on her nest as she had done so many times before. She sat there for two hours, hopped down, and came away singing. In the meantime, HHH was sitting on the nest in the black plastic bucket in the hen house. She too got down from her bucket nest and seemed to be very proud of herself. Barney looked, and in the bucket nest he saw an egg.

"So it was HHH," he exclaimed, but returning to the house, he looked again into the garage. There he saw Little Grey Hen and Little Red Rooster sitting on the handles of the wheelbarrow, and in a rounded out nest in the grass clippings in the wheelbarrow was one little white egg.

"Now what?" he said, turning to Taffy, and then to Max, neither of whom was giving him any help. "Which one laid first? Always a mystery with these little chickens."

TALE SEVEN: ONE NEST: HOW MANY HENS?

B arney's brother James came to visit him. James came from St. Augustine and he drove all the way without stopping to sleep. "I will be there at two thirty in the afternoon," he told Barney, but he arrived early in the morning instead, and he could not find Barney because Barney had gone to the laundry, and when he came home he found James sitting in his car on the driveway.

"I was afraid you'd had a stroke and were lying in there on the floor." James said, hugging his younger brother.

"Worse than that," Barney replied. "I was washing the sheets in celebration of your coming. You see how much I honor you."

James wanted to get on with the business of their visit. "We will drive to Missouri tomorrow to see our brother Joe."

"Joe can wait. Let me show you my chickens. I'll bet you never saw anything like this." Then Barney showed James the three little hens on one nest with six eggs under them. James stood open mouthed at this spectacle.

"Never in my eighty six years," he said "have I seen three hens on one nest. What will happen?"

"I was counting on you to tell me that, Elder Brother. But we go to Missouri tomorrow, and the next day those eggs will crack open and the baby chicks will be waiting for us when we get back."

And that is just what happened when the two brothers returned from Missouri. Barney hurried to the hen house without unpacking his bag. He raised up the three little hens and found five baby chicks and one egg under them.

"Hey. What happens now? How will we divide the babies?" Barney looked at his brother James. But neither Barney nor his brother James had the answer. Mother Nature had the answer though. She had spoken to the three little hens. And when Barney set them all on the floor, with the five brown and yellow striped babies, Hen Number One spreading her wings and making a fan of her tail feathers, and fluffing up the feathers all over her body and making the feathers on her neck stand up, let it be known that she was the mother hen. Then Hen Number Two, standing nearby and clucking urgently, attempted to get the baby chicks to believe that she was their mother. And Hen Number Three flew back onto the nest and settled on the one unhatched egg. The babies went to Hen Number One. Except one baby who stood, undecided, then ran to Hen Number Two.

Barney said "Now you all have names, and he called Hen Number One Fulfilled. Hen Number Two became Frustrated. And Hen Number Three, Hopeful. The five baby chicks ran about cheeping and wondering what to eat. Barney went inside his kitchen and cooked up a batch of rice and egg whites for their first meal.

On the second day after Barney's return from Missouri his brother James left before sunup and Barney stood amazed in the presence of all the new life he saw scurrying about on the floor of the hen house. Fulfilled was fluffed out twice her normal size, and she was teaching the babies to eat rice and egg whites. She clucked, picked up a grain of rice and dropped it in front of a chick who picked it up and swallowed it. Frustrated was hovering inside the hiding place under the washtub with the black plastic bucket nests up above it. One chick had stayed with her, but she was unhappy about this uneven and unfair division. And Hopeful was still sitting, bright eyed, on the one unhatched egg.

Then a threat arose. "It could be a real tragedy," Barney said, "If a snake..." For Barney had opened the hen house door to let the cocks and the big grey hen run free in the yard. They had come cackling, fluttering, crowing for how wonderful freedom is. But they were not the only ones to run for freedom.

When he looked back, Fulfilled, together with Frustrated, had come out too, and they were followed by the five baby chicks. "I didn't think those little fellows would leave the safety of their cave." But Barney stood watching, as the mother hens, clucking to the cheeping baby chicks, ran under the Forsythia bush.

And all went well, until ... yes, until the time came for the babies to go back into the hen house and to their safe cave under the wash tub. For night was coming on and Barney grew concerned because Mother Hen Number One, that's Fulfilled, would not bring them out from under the Forsythia bush, but planned to settle down under that thick, leafy covering for the night. "But a snake will get them there" Barney exclaimed. "Or a varmint. But surely a snake." And he could see the picture in his mind's eye. A BIG BLACK SNAKE swallowing the five baby chicks while the helpless mother hens ruffled their feathers and maybe even pecked at the snake but were unable to stop him. Then five bumps showing in the long sluggish body of the snake. Frightening.

But how to get the mother hens and the baby chicks from under the Forsythia bush? For it was impossible for Barney to penetrate and get inside. So he poked at it with his walking stick and shook the branches and called to the hens and their babies. Finally, Frustrated came out, with one chick following her. Then a second chick, yellow with brown stripes, followed her too. But three chicks remained with Fulfilled who refused to come out from the bush.

Instead, she gathered the three baby chicks under her wings and settled down for the night under the Forsythia bush. Barney turned to Taffy and said "Well, that's the way it is ... Unless she will come out." And he went to sit on the front porch with his feet on the door steps. He picked up Thomas Wolfe's Look Homeward Angel, and tried to read. Taffy and Max watched him, and he said to them "When it gets dark..." But he did not know what he could do when it got dark, so he went back to look, and he found that Fulfilled had brought the chicks to the edge of the bush near the hen house and had sat down on them. "Yes, when it get's dark, I will throw the flashlight beam in her eyes and take them all in the hen house."

So he went back to Look Homeward Angel and waited for darkness. But darkness comes slowly in late May, when you are waiting for it. So he went back and tried to pick the hen up with one hand and the baby chicks with the other. The hen squawked and kicked up a row, and the baby chicks ran back under the bush. "All right. All right."

He set Fulfilled down and she went back under the bush to find the chicks. Then hen and chicks went out the other side of the bush and headed toward the hen house, but

Taffy came at that moment. She barked once at what she saw coming from under the Forsythia bush and the hen and chicks ran under again.

Barney called to Taffy and put her on the leash. "You are not being helpful," he told her. He sat down on the steps and picked up Look Homeward Angel, but he had lost his place in it, so he went back to the Forsythia bush. Fulfilled had settled again over her three chicks, while Frustrated had taken her two to the cave, and was quarreling about the other hen and chicks. Barney tried again. This time Fulfilled got up and headed for the hen house, the chicks following.

Fulfilled bustled into the hen house; the chicks were in hot pursuit. And Barney threw a beam of light, and soon the two hens and five chicks were settled into the cave under the wash tub. And Hopeful was sitting on the unhatched egg in the black plastic bucket nest. "Well, thank Goodness that's over ... for the night, anyway." Barney let Taffy off the leash. He popped a can of Nine Lives which brought Max running into the house. "We've foiled the snake." He said it almost in a whisper, lest the snake hear him. Then he settled down with Look Homeward Angel and said, "Now where did I leave off?"

Next morning at daybreak Barney went with boiled rice and egg white to feed the chicks. They did not respond to his voice, but they came running out in response to Fulfilled's clucking. He let the cocks and the big grey hen out into the yard, looked into the cave and found Frustrated hiding there with one chick. Hopeful was sitting tight on her egg. He set the pan of rice and egg white down. Fulfilled showed it to the baby chicks, and Barney went back to the kitchen for a cup of coffee. Max was waiting for him there. He started to tell Max that they had outwitted the snake, but Max was not interested, nor concerned about snakes and their appetite for baby chicks.

Now the five baby chicks were five days old, and on that fifth day of their lives Fulfilled introduced them to a new adventure. She led them out into the hen yard where she began scratching in the litter and pecking at things too small for Barney to see. But not too small for the baby chicks. Anyway, they pecked too. "So they must be seeing something ... but wait a minute. What's this? I see only four chicks."

He went back into the hen house. There was Frustrated, with one baby chick, hiding under the wash tub. Barney set the plate of rice on the floor and called to Fulfilled. She came, four babies tumbling into the hen house after her. The one baby who had remained with Frustrated looked up and saw what was happening. He abandoned his unhappy mother and ran to join the pack. For that was where the food was.

Then Hopeful flew down from the nest where the unhatched egg lay. She started clucking and showing the babies how to eat rice and egg white. She was running about very busily and aggressively, to the discomfiture of both Fulfilled and Frustrated. And all five babies were now feasting, with no evident concern for the unfair division of labors between their three mothers, but running back and forth like small children at a birthday party with three sets of parents vying with one another for their favor.

Hopeful has given up hope; she is now Hopeless. Perhaps it is better to say that she has given up hope on that one unhatched egg, and she is getting ready for a new life. In any case, Hopeful/Hopeless has now abandoned that egg. Thrown it out onto the floor of the hen house.

Barney broke the egg and found that the yellow and the white had run together and mixed. He threw it away. "No good." He looked at Taffy. "That egg would never hatch if she sat on it forever."

Hopeful/Hopeless is now running free in the yard, and the cocks are showing an interest in her. They find little tidbits and goodies in the grass. They scratch and cluck, calling to her. "Oh come and see what I have found. See how smart I am. Don't you want to mate with me?" And she no longer runs around with her feathers fluffed out like a mother hen. She hugs her feathers smoothly to her trim, lithe body. Can there be a new romance in the offing?

So Hopeful/Hopeless has now become Hope Reborn. She will soon be laying eggs again; she may even be getting her own brood started. But Fulfilled continues to fluff her feathers out so that she appears bigger than she really is. This impresses Frustrated, and Frustrated does not dare to challenge her, but she does not give up her claim to the chicks either. Frustrated stands off at a safe distance and clucks to the baby chicks. They run to her because they want to know what she has found; they have no sense of loyalty to Fulfilled. So Frustrated may be coming up for a renaming too. Barney has not decided what it will be though. Frustrated/Hanging in there? And Loyalty?

Tale Eight: Finally An Egg

"The Little Grey Hen has laid an egg." Barney made this announcement to Taffy and Max. They received the news without any outward show of emotion. Taffy lay on the concrete floor of the front porch. A sleepy expression in her eyes. Her mouth standing open. Panting because of the heat. Moisture dripping from her tongue and lips. Max stretched himself lazily on the floor, but he was watchful because Taffy's seeming unconcern might be a trap. "I said," Barney repeated, "the Little Grey Hen has laid an egg. What she has been practising for. What the Little Red Rooster has been waiting for. I think both of them would like for me to have an item on it in the newspaper."

It was indeed an event worth telling. And on the next day there were two eggs in the straw in the rusty old metal box on the shelf at the rear of the garage where Barney had piled oil cans and gasoline containers and rat traps and God knows what all. Two eggs now lie in that nest in the straw, and Little Grey Hen has become the object of the attention and desire of all the cocks in the yard. The two larger cocks have become very aggressive about it.

The two larger cocks have teamed up on the Little Red Rooster. He can stand off one of them, but then the other comes, and together they drive him away. Then both of them begin to chase the Little Grey Hen. They want to mate with her. But she is having none of it. She does not want to mate with these two. Frightened, she comes running to Barney for protection. Then, flying up onto the hood of Barney's old antique car, she has found an effective escape for even if they fly up there too, they can't get an adequate purchase on the smooth metal to accomplish the mating act. Frustrated, they circle one another on the ground, scratching their wings with their toe nails, crowing lustily. The Little Red Rooster stands at a distance, waiting.

At last the two cocks go away; it is no use waiting; there are other hens. Little Grey Hen flies down onto the ground to be joined again by the Little Red Rooster who clucks and calls her to come and see what he has found for her. He circles her, scratches his wing, letting her know that he is her rightful husband. She sings happily; she has now been delivered from rape by the two larger roosters. All is quiet in Barney's yard now … for the moment anyway.

Turning to Taffy, Barney says "She is faithful."

Taffy's eyes, her face, seemed to be laughing. Her eyes said "Scared. She's scared of those two big roosters."

"Whatever … It's time for me to drive them into the hen house now anyway. They've made enough trouble for one day."

The warm days of June passed and on the first day of July, Barney announced to Taffy and Max. "She's pregnant. The Little Grey Hen is brooding. Sitting on seven eggs in the nest in the old metal box on the shelf in the garage. Yes, there she sits amid the junk of oil cans, old batteries, rat traps and a dozen other bits of used and unused litter. And what do you think the Little Red Rooster is doing?"

Taffy turned knowing eyes on Barney, and Barney said "You guessed it, Or did you see? He's sidling up to that buff colored hen. Not losing any time, is he? Cocky little fellow. He's put her on to hatch the next brood of babies and now he's looking around. But his attention is divided. Look at him now, sitting on the wheelbarrow handles, like an expectant father in the waiting room."

It is now the seventh day of the seventh month of this year two thousand and three, and Barney stood in the garage, gazing at the Little Grey Hen on her nest in the old metal box. Dedicated to her job of brooding on those eggs, she had settled onto them seven days ago, and had not moved from the nest since that day. Neither food nor water, nor the company of the other chickens in the flock, could lure her from that nest. Neither heat nor boredom could drive her from her close place there.

Barney extended his hand to touch her; she pecked him, quarreling at this intrusion. The Little Red Rooster is lonesome. He watches from a nearby perch on the handle of the wheelbarrow. Barney had filled the wheelbarrow with grass clippings from the lawn, and the lonesome little cock had made a nest in the grass clippings, as if he hoped that his mate would come and lay an egg there. But it was an empty gesture, as empty as the nest he had made. Now he runs back and forth across the yard, fleeing his own loneliness, but afraid to approach the other chickens because of the two larger cocks. Now he stands on top of the bird feeding station – a rustic board nailed onto the top of a post and he crows lustily, answering the two cocks in the henyard, even challenging them from this safe distance.

Scratching Taffy's ears and looking into the future, Barney said "Well Old Girl, a fortnight now and we will have a new batch of babies, if that little mother doesn't starve herself to death."

Taffy turned limpid eyes on Barney. "A fortnight is two weeks," he added. "Fourteen days and nights." Taffy was not impressed by this translation. Her eyes said "I know how long it takes for eggs to hatch. Nobody has to tell me. Twenty one days. But you can tell that to your readers."

Barney gazed at Taffy, wondering how she came to have such knowledge, and again her eyes spoke to him. "I was born knowing what you have to learn from reading books. I know how long it takes to make puppies too. Even though somebody tricked me out of the pleasure of my birthright when I was a pup, the knowledge is still there."

"You are a very smart little lady, Taffy. How long does it take?"

"Sixty three days."

Time drags for the Little Red Rooster, and it is now the eighth day of July. Little Grey Hen sits bright eyed on her eggs, and Little Red Rooster's eye is wandering. He has noticed Frustrated, who is now the sole mother of the young chicks who follow her about the yard and into the edge of the corn field. Boldly, he approaches, and knowing that the maternal instinct is strong, he begins playing Papa to the four half grown pullets and one cockerel, clucking and calling them to come and see what wonders he has uncovered in the grass and in the edge of the corn field. His faithful brooding mate is sitting on those eggs that hold the promise of the future. She will not leave them, even though Little Red Rooster's eye is roving. Barney moves the pan of water and the food close so that she can reach them without leaving the nest. She ignores even this act of kindness on his part.

"Dedication." Barney says to Taffy. "Now that is dedication. But Little Red Rooster? I am beginning to suspect that he is a bounder."

On the ninth day of July the Little Red Rooster pushed his luck beyond its limits. Barney had noticed him scratching his wing and circling Frustrated, but now as evening came on, and the chickens were all running for the hen house, Little Red Rooster followed Frustrated and her half grown chicks right into the hen yard, and there, for one glorious moment he stood triumphant. Then the bigger cocks, who had gone into the hen house, saw him and they came crashing out into the hen yard, attacked Little Red Rooster, and drove him ignominiously from the hen yard. He fled toward the garage and his perch on top of the old piano.

"Vanquished," Barney said to Max who was watching it all while crouching in the classic pose of the leon couchant. "Frustrated himself now in his first attempt to be unfaithful to his mate … Well, Old Fellow, you just let that be a lesson to you, and maybe I won't tell on you. But I can't speak for Max and Taffy. They may just give it all away … Well, come on Taffy. It's hot out here."

The next day, the tenth, was a very special day for Barney. His friends Bill and Betty had come for coffee, and they wanted to see the Banties. So Barney broke precedent and let the whole flock out of the hen house at midmorning so that his friends could admire them as they ran to check the bird feeders under the maple trees in the back yard. "What beauties," Bill and Betty exclaimed. But as soon as Frustrated and her brood of five were strung out across the lawn, Little Red Rooster came out of the garage and made a mad dash to join them. But the two larger cocks saw him and gave chase again. He fled in terror.

"That Little Red Rooster has a problem," Bill observed.

"Yes," Barney replied. "But it's one we can't help him with. Let's go and have another cup of coffee, and wish him luck."

TALE NINE: A PAUSE
FOR REFLECTION

Barney stood on the driveway littered with chicken feathers. "What's happened here?" Anxious now, he went away to the hen house and counted. Yes. One was missing. One of the Big Grey Hens. He went back to study the evidence of violence. Violence that had occurred right under his nose. Even while he sat relaxed and reading, in the house. No sound had reached his ears. Not a squawk. Not a cackle. Not the flutter of wings. Had the struggle been silent? But there were the feathers on the ground. And the Big Grey Hen was gone.

Barney studied the crime scene. He reflected. "Could it be Jim's old black dog? It just has to be. I'll kill him ... if I catch him at it."

But how could he catch Old Blackie, the shaggy black dog who came every day to visit Taffy? To nose about the place, and then continue on his rounds of the neighborhood. A quiet, friendly, unobtrusive old fellow. Barney had referred to him as "Taffy's black boy friend." If Barney was in the house when Old Blackie came, she would allow him free run of the place. Even the privilege of sniffing her. But not much. And if Barney walked out and became witness to what was going on, she would growl and bark and drive Old

Blackie away. And now a hen was killed on the driveway. Feathers scattered all the way to the garage doors. "And the two little cocks are not yet accounted for." Barney was angry; his adrenaline was up.

How? So long as the chickens were in the chicken house, nothing would happen to them. To catch Old Blackie in the act, he would have to turn the chickens out again. "And risk the loss of another one?" he asked himself. Certainly, he couldn't let them run loose on the yard while he lolled about inside the house, reading a book. He would have to be out there, watching. Even while he watched, Old Blackie could walk in quietly, as if he had no interest in the chickens, then launch a sudden attack, and there would be another dead chicken. "I have already lost two cocks, and now this hen. It's a risk. Do I want to take this chance in order to prove my suspicion? To be able to say it's Old Blackie. He's the culprit. A chicken killing dog."

"And if I catch him at the killing job, and I shoot him, what then? Will I drag him over to my neighbor's house and say I have killed your dog?"

Barney picked up a grey chicken feather and studied it. "Jim is a good neighbor. He once saved my house from burning. I had left a pile of trash burning in the back yard, then gone off to town, and returned to find Jim out there fighting fire." He had been alarmed by Taffy's barking, and found the fire before it reached the garage and the house.

"And even if I were not in his debt, a neighbor is a neighbor. And the quickest route to changing a good neighbor into a bad enemy is to shoot his dog." Barney turned the feather over between his fingers, Taffy looked up into his face. He said "and then there is Taffy."

Barney studied Taffy's face. "And if I shoot my neighbor's dog, he may shoot mine. The matter of his dog's guilt won't

46

even enter into it if he becomes angry over what I have done. Retaliation will be the name of the game. But is there not a better way to handle it?"

Reflecting. "So what if I go to him now, before the dog gets another chicken, and say to him, I believe your dog is killing my chickens? Then he will say to me What proof do you have that my dog is killing your chickens? Have you found feathers in his mouth? And I will have to admit that I have no proof. And what have I accomplished? I have awakened suspicion. And made things bad with my neighbor. So the solution is worse than the problem I am trying to solve."

Stooping to pat Taffy on the head, Barney gave up the idea of doing anything about Old Blackie. "So I will look somewhere else for the guilty party. Look up." Now he stood up and tilted his head back, his eyes searching the sky. "Maybe it was a hawk. Yes, the killer came from the sky. Dived onto the hen, knocked her over. She struggled and dragged the hawk toward the garage. But the hawk held on, tearing the feathers out all the way. Never releasing its talons from the hen's flesh. The prey is conquered, captured. The hawk lifts off the ground, bearing its prize, flies away to some bare tree limb in the woods where it eats flesh, feathers, bones, all. Nothing is left for me to find. But he will come back when he is hungry again, and I will shoot him. Yes, I'll turn the chickens out again, and watch for the hawk."

TALE TEN: MYSTERY OF
THE MISSING COCKS

I t is a mystery beyond understanding and Barney is indeed mystified.

"Little Red! Golden Boy! Where are you?" Barney called from the open garage door. He called and called. But there was no answer from Little Red and Golden Boy. Only the Little Grey Hen answered with her peculiar sing song clucking sound. It was a sad, lonesome sound of lostness. Little Hen ran out from under the antique car. She came to the feed pan where Barney was dumping fresh feed. Fear shone in her eyes. Where were Little Red and Golden Boy?

Barney had been away from home for two days. He was visiting a friend in Detroit. Barney and his friend Mike talked and talked and talked, for it had been a long time, and there was much to talk about. They rode about the area where Mike had been born, had lived as a boy, and where his parents and family members still live. "Over there…" Mike would say. "Now under this bridge…" and "see this old house up ahead." Or "Here is where I…"

A little farther on Barney saw the little huts out on the ice covered lake. "What are they doing out there on the ice?"

"Fishing."

"Fishing in the ice?"

"Through a hole in the ice."

"And all those boats sitting ten feet up in the air and none in the water?"

"Everybody here has a boat but nobody can leave his boat in the water in winter. The boat would be crushed by the ice when the water freezes."

"It is a strange world here on the lake." Barney said. But Mike was eager to show Barney the hospital where he worked. So they left the frozen lake with the fishermen in their little huts scattered about on the ice, and they drove back to town and to the hospital. Mike worked in the department of spiritual care for the hospital had been started by religious sisters who were concerned for both physical and spiritual health. And Mike's work was very important because he was a comforter to the people in pain and afraid of what might happen to them. Then Barney remembered that when he was young he himself did this kind of work, and was happy and fulfilled in it. He remembered the woman who had asked him what a chaplain does except go about and hold people's hands when they are sick.

"Is there anything else to do that is more important than that?" Barney had replied. For when people are sick and afraid and do not know what is going to happen to them … But then Barney thought again of his little dog Taffy and the yellow cat Max who would be lonely and afraid because he was not there with them. So Barney and Mike ate in unusual restaurants, and they talked of the things they were doing and of those whom they loved, and

Barney said "I have to go home to Taffy and Max. And my little chickens."

Mike knew about Taffy and Max, but he did not know about the chickens. And Barney said "It is cold. Freezing. Their water turns to ice so quickly. I have to go home."

Mike and Barney drove together to the airport where Barney boarded a plane for Nashville, after showing his identification seven times, and when the plane landed he got into his car and drove home, going first to the Animal Clinic where he was reunited with Taffy. She was so happy to see him that she sat up on the car seat and barked all the way home where Max was waiting for him in Barney's reclining chair. Max made low mewing sounds and he wanted to be held in Barney's arms. Then Barney went to see the chickens, but something had happened. Little Red and Golden Boy were not there when he opened the garage door to look for them. They were gone. Vanished. Without leaving a feather as evidence of what had happened to them.

Barney searched the garage, he searched the tool shed, he looked under the Forsythia bush, and he peered into the Privet clump. He looked up at the roofs of the garage and the hen house. His eyes searched the trees standing tall in the yard. The surrounding fields and the hedgerows. Even the edge of a nearby woodland. He called to Little Red and Golden Boy, but there was no answer.

Over and over Barney searched every place where he thought the two little cocks could be. And he called and called but there was no answer to his call. Then he went back into the garage to look again. Only the Little Grey Hen was there, lonely, and timid with fear in her eyes. She came near to him and looked up at his face, but he could not read what was in her eyes, and she could not tell him what had happened to Little Red and Golden Boy.

The cocks in the hen house crowed, but there was no answer to them from the missing cocks. The Little Grey Hen made her clucking sing song sound, but it was sad and lonely and lost. Night came on. And the night was followed by morning. Still there was no sound of the familiar voices. In the place where Little Red and Golden Boy had been, there was silence. The place did not seem the same without the crowing of Little Red and Golden Boy in the garage, for when the cocks in the hen house crowed there was no response. In his mind's eye Barney could see the two little cocks flapping their wings and throwing back their heads and expanding their throats, but it was only in the mind's eye, and it is difficult to express the emptiness created by the absence of sound.

The sound of a cock's crowing, greeting the dawn of a new day, urging the sun to come up over the eastern horizon, answering the challenge of the cocks in the hen house. Each morning after Little Red and Golden Boy disappeared, Barney awakened, listening, and he got up from his bed before daylight, to look out on the snow covered landscape, to listen for the old familiar sound that was no longer there. He listened and listened, straining to hear the familiar sound, but there was nothing to hear.

"This is a mystery wrapped in an enigma," Barney said to Taffy, who looked back at him with sad, moist eyes. "It is a puzzle I can't unravel," he said to Max, and Max rubbed himself against Barney's feet. And to the Little Grey Hen who came running with her sing song of loneliness, he said "I cannot plumb the depths of this loss. It is a mystery too deep for me. I feel the loneliness I see in your eyes and hear in your little sing song, but I cannot understand."

Barney took the Little Grey Hen in his hands and held her close. He took her to the hen house and placed her on the roost pole beside the other chickens, but when morning came and she was discovered, the hens of the flock pecked her and drove her into a corner where she cowered in terror. Barney lifted her out of the close place where she was hiding, and took her back to the empty garage.

How can a garage be empty with two cars and a lawn mower in it? It can be empty by the unexplained disappearance of two little cocks who were handsome and brave but beaten, and had found a friendship with one another because both of them were driven out of the flock by the more dominant roosters.

On the sixth day of his return Barney went for the second time that morning to replace the ice with warm water in the cup set out for the Little Grey Hen, and at first he could not see her, but as he was leaving the tool shed he saw her red comb raised above the edge of the cardboard box with wheat straw in it for a nest. An hour later he returned, opened the door, and looked into the box. The nest was empty. No egg. The Little Grey Hen had sought some instinctive, primeval source of comfort in the nest. Then, not finding it, she had gone again to hide under the old car. But the mystery of the disappearance of Little Red and Golden Boy remains unsolved.

Did a fox or a coyote sweep through the yard and catch them unawares? Did a neighbor's dog chase them down and carry them off? Did a hawk drop out of the sky and seize them in its talons? Did some nocturnal predator find them on the roost? And all without leaving a feather?

Or did some human thief come, knowing that Barney was away from home, and carry away his prized and precious cocks?

TALE ELEVEN: HOW MANY
HENS ON ONE HEN'S NEST?

"Now just look here." Barney's surprise showed on his face and in his voice. Taffy looked, with round bright, expectant eyes. "I do believe this little banty hen is broody. Yessirree. No doubt about it."

This little banty hen with the bright beady eyes was immobile on the nest, but when Barney moved near her, she puffed up her feathers, squawked at him, and her bright beady eyes said "I shall not be moved from this place."

All the other hens, and the cocks as well, were scurrying about the hen house, cackling excitedly. But not this little yellow brown hen. She was sitting tight. "Well now, this is news ... I hadn't expected ... but ... then this is Spring."

True. It was Spring. And the little banty hen with the high red comb and the bright beady eyes, obedient to the call of Mother Nature, had taken her place in the big black plastic bucket nest that Barney had fastened to the roost pole in the corner of the hen house. It was the South East corner, and she would not be moved.

Barney extended his right hand tentatively toward the little hen. She swelled up, puffed out her feathers, complained querulously, and pecked his hand. "That for you," her bright beady eyes said to Barney.

"Ouch." Barney drew his hand back quickly. A red spot appeared on his hand and he rubbed it with the other hand. "Pecked me. A feisty little mother, you are." He turned to Taffy who was sitting at his feet, watching. She yipped. What did her yip mean? "Let me at her. I'll show her."

"I guess she means business," Barney commented to Taffy. "But what are we going to do about this? It sort of upsets things in here."

What could Barney do? Mother Nature sends a message to a little banty hen. She says to the little banty hen "It's time. Time for you to become a mother, along with me. Responsibility. No more running carefree about the yard, picking greens and scratching in the litter in the corn field. It is time for you to get serious about the business of life. Time to brood."

Still rubbing his hand where the hen had pecked him, Barney walked quickly to the house. Taffy followed. Max watched from his place under the Maple tree. In the kitchen, Barney opened the refrigerator door, peered in. Counted the eggs. Six in one bowl. Five in another. "That ought to be enough ... But will they hatch? That is the question."

Taffy looked back at him with bright black eyes. Her eyes said "that is not the question. The question is, What are you going to do with those eggs? They are for our breakfast."

Barney closed the refrigerator door and said "I will have to ask somebody." At the Sunrise Cafe next morning, Barney asked the lady who runs the restaurant. "No," she said. "The eggs in the fridge won't hatch. Forty five degrees kills them. You will have to use fresh eggs that have never been in the fridge."

Barney went home and began the search for fresh eggs. He found two in another nest in the hen house, and one new one under the hen on her nest. Placing the three eggs in a bowl on the cabinet, Barney turned to Taffy and Max. "There will be more. Patience." Patience is Max's specialty. Curiosity is too. He mewed and wondered what Barney was doing with the eggs.

Next day he found two more freshly laid eggs. "All right, Five it is. Here we go." He slipped them one by one under the quarreling hen. She tucked them under her warm body, settled herself over her treasure, and stared back at Barney with bright beady eyes. Taffy sat watching this operation with wonderment. "Mine" the bright beady eyes said. "Keep that dog out of here."

Max came up and watched the hens and cocks who were watching Barney and Taffy. The chickens were nervous. They stretched their necks. The hens cackled and the cocks crowed, Max excited them even more by crouching and staring at them. His tail would have twitched if he had a tail but he had no tail because Max is a Manx cat, so his long body quivered and he crouched and stared.

Barney walked slowly back toward the house. "Come on you two. I can see that you plan to make trouble out here." In the kitchen he found a calendar on the breakfast table. "Now let me see. It is the twenty third of April." He marked that date with a big S. Turning to Taffy, he said, "that means Set. The day I set the eggs under the hen. Now, count twenty one days." He found May fourteen and marked it with a big H. "Hatch Day. That's the day we will see baby chicks breaking out of their egg shells."

Taffy and Max watched and pretended to be listening. Taffy is deaf, so it did not matter much what Barney said. And Max had his mind on other things. But Barney was suspicious of those two. "I will have to watch you. One bite and you would gobble up a baby chick." He went back to have another look at the brooding hen and he was surprised to see that there were now two hens on the nest.

"Now just look at this. Both hens ruffled up their feathers and quarreled at him for disturbing them. What to make of this? Barney was surprised.

"What's going on here now? Two hens sitting in here now." Two bright beady eyes were staring at him. And one bunch of tail feathers, for one hen was turned out and the other was turned in. "But this complicates things. Who's going to be the mother when...?"

Then another complication. More eggs than the five he had placed under the hen. Now six. The next day seven. "They won't all hatch at the same time if this goes on." So Barney opened his ball point pen and made little circular markings on the eggs. Next day he found eight eggs, and removed the one that had no mark on it. "So. That other little banty hen is slipping in here and laying her eggs with the broody hens. Just wait until I catch her..." He opened the hen house door, and all the chickens ran out, except the two broody hens on the nest. Soon they too fluffed themselves up, quarreled, and hopped down and ran out into the yard. They were very self important and the other hens and cocks stayed out of their way.

Two days later. Another surprise. Three little hens crowded into the nest, all three of them fluffed out and quarreling at Barney. The little yellow hen was jammed in between the other two. Very carefully, Barney lifted them all off, one at a time, and set them on the floor, counted the eggs and found eight again. He removed the unmarked one. "This is just too much," Barney remarked to Taffy and Max. They agreed with him. Taffy made a pass at the whole flock and sent them flying and cackling. Max crouched and waited, hoping one of the smaller ones would come close enough for him to make a catch. Barney called to both Max and Taffy. He went to the front porch, sat down and started to read Thomas Wolfe's LOOK HOMEWARD ANGEL. At sundown, he went to close up the chicken house. The little yellow hen had driven the other two hens out of the nest. The two evicted hens were sitting on the roost pole, looking very unhappy about the situation. Then, six days before the scheduled hatch, Barney found that bad luck had struck. All three hens were on the nest, pushing against one another and scrambling with their feet. One egg had been broken and a dead chick, cast out into the world before his time, lay among the eggs. He removed the dead chick, removed two more unmarked eggs, and went away, saddened.

At nightfall, the three little hens were lined up on the nest, two heads and one tail pointing out. Barney closed the door on this strange nest of hens and eggs.

Four days before Hatch Day, Barney found the little yellow hen sitting on the roost pole. She was unhappy. The two other hens had driven her out, but she was not giving up. "Trouble," Barney said. "Trouble for the latest interloper. I will try something." He took two eggs from under the two hens on the nest, placed the eggs in another nest, took the little evicted hen and placed her on the nest with the two eggs. She became excited, flew off, refusing to have anything to do with this new nest. He replaced the eggs under the two brooding hens. "All right. Have it your own way." He went back to Thomas Wolfe's LOOK HOMEWARD ANGEL. "The ways of Mother Nature are beyond my powers of comprehension."

At last account, the late comer, the little yellow hen, was sitting on the roost pole, waiting, hoping, for what? That one of the two hens on the nest would get hungry enough to vacate a spot big enough for her to slip in and realize her destiny. In the meantime Barney was wondering: What will happen when I go to visit my brother in Missouri? That is when the eggs are scheduled to hatch. Will the three mothers be able to handle matters until I come home?

Tale Twelve: Little Chickens Celebrate St. Patrick's Day

On St. Patrick's Day the sun rose like the great ball of fire that it is. The air was a bit nippy, as it is in mid March, and a breeze soon rose, brisk too, as breezes are at that time of year. And Barney, having set the coffee pot to perking, hastened out to the chicken house to return the greetings already arising there. For the young roosters were challenging the old one with raucous crowing, and the old one was answering the young ones with contempt and threats. Even that young rooster, did we name him Twelfth or Dozenth? That lone chick now grown to a size soon to challenge the very biggest of the young cocks, yes, he too was crowing proudly, and beginning to grow some tail feathers as further proof of his maleness.

Barney took sunflower seeds and cracked corn with wheat mixed in, and water too. All the Little Chickens looked up expectantly at Barney when he opened the door with his hands full of food and drink. He counted them. Once. Twice. Three times. For they kept moving about, and what is so hard to count as chickens moving about? But yes, they were all there. Twelve of them. Six cocks and six hens. All alive and safe, and eager for the new day, and food and water, and to be heard.

"What a fine flock!" Barney exulted. "Nobody else in this whole community has such a flock of beauties. Oh, there are chicken farms. Hundreds of chickens. Maybe even thousands. But they are chickens being raised for the market. To be eaten. But that's different. I would not consider letting my Little Chickens be eaten. Someone once suggested that I eat them. What a terrible thing to suggest. They are my pets. They are my...my...my CHILDREN. I could not eat them."

The day grew warmer, although the wind grew stronger, and the sun high in the sky did not seem so miraculous as when it was rising over the treetops beyond the bean field. And Barney's thoughts returned repeatedly to the Little Chickens. So much so that he lost interest in Anthony Trollope's story of the Eustace Diamonds, and he returned to crop green grass at the edge of the yard where the farmer's bean field joined his lawn. Clumps of green were growing there and Barney wrenched the leaves easily, dropped them into a plastic bucket, and took them to the chicken pen, where he let the green leaves of grass fall through the wire covering onto the ground in the pen. The Little Chickens rushed to pick them up, thinking what a treat it was to have green grass added to their regular diet of sunflower and grain. Surely Spring had come with all its promise.

In the late afternoon Barney made his decision. "Spring Treat! That's what it will be. "And he opened the hen house door. "Come on out. It's Saint Patrick's Day. Come out and celebrate Spring!" And out they came in a stream. Running and cackling with glee. Excitement was in their moving bodies, and in their exultant hearts. Never has anyone seen a happier flock of Little Chickens. Happiness reigned supreme. Cocks and hens raced over the back yard. Barney stood admiring them, then he had a thought. "I'd better bring my gun out here. I remember that hawk who came and stared hungrily at them. And I remember my neighbor's old black dog who carried off Little Red. Well, I won't shoot the hawk for I don't want to go to prison. And I won't shoot Old Blackie because his owner is my neighbor, and that's no way to make neighbors. But if they come, I'll shoot into the air and give them a good scare."

So Barney brought his gun, and the book too because he thought he might read while the Little Chickens ran about over the yard. And a metal folding chair to sit on. And his walking stick. He called it his third leg. And with all this he was equipped to watch and protect his Little Chickens. Then Taffy came, saying with her eyes, "You'll need me too, to watch them and keep them out of mischief."

Spring Break in the Back Yard! A true Holiday. A picnic. They're finding all sorts of treats invisible to the human eye. And of course they've discovered SEX. At least the cocks have!" For they were trying determinedly to mount the squawking, resisting hens. And Little Grey Hen, the Matriarch of the flock, is maintaining a modicum of decency. She rules both cocks and pullets, and she gives both of the cocks a severe peck to let them know to stay in their place. But what's this? Little Brownie, a brown and yellow speckled young hen, lately a pullet who has begun to lay an occasional egg, has found something unusual.

What is it? A small mouse or mole? A baby bird fallen prematurely from a too early nest? A tiny frog responding early to the Spring sunshine? Whatever, it is something new, special, and as soon as she has it, all the others see and want it. So now they are all chasing her to take the prize from her, and she is fleeing desperately. For her life? Well, definitely for her prize. Back and forth she races across the yard, her pursuers hard upon her heels. Then Taffy takes note of the commotion, and she decides its outcome. Rushing into the flock, she barks once, and sends the Little Chickens flying in all directions. Little Brownie holds onto her prize, runs under the Forsythia bush, swallows it, and emerges stretching her neck. Relative quiet has returned, and Taffy looks at Barney. "Right, Old Girl! That situation called for a watchful watch dog to restore Law and Order."

Suddenly, the hormones kicked in with the young cocks. Golden Boy Junior was trying to mount one of the little brown hens. Then Castor and Pollux, the two young red roosters with brown speckles on their breasts, squared off to fight it out over possession of the whole flock. Neck feathers ruffled, eyes fierce, beaks open, wings at half spread, they flew at one another, pecking and hitting. The old red rooster noticed. He came and broke up the fight. "I'm in charge here. If there's any fighting to be done, I'll do it." The young cocks went back to searching for goodies among the leaves at the edge of the garden fence.

Night was coming. Chickens go to roost early. Even Little Chickens on holiday. Barney wanted to watch the evening news, but he did not dare leave the Little Chickens unattended. "Come on Taffy. Let's get these birds back in the house." He herded the Little Chickens through the open door of the hen house. All except Castor. Castor had not fared well in his encounter with Pollux. Now he was reluctant to go inside and risk a second run in with his brother. Castor ran past the open door. He ran around the corner of the chicken pen, cackling excitedly. Barney and Taffy came after him, and drove him to the open door. He ran in, looking back over his shoulder at Barney and Taffy, then flew up onto the roost pole, still cackling over his adventure.

"End of a perfect day!" Barney exulted, and Taffy yipped her agreement.

TALE THIRTEEN: THE CHICKEN HAWK

"Corn Bread!" Barney said to the attractive waitress at the restaurant. "Corn Bread is what I'll have with my lunch." But when the lunch came, a meat and three vegetables, and corn bread, Barney wrapped the corn bread in a paper napkin, and slipped it into his trouser pocket. "For Taffy," he said to his friend Bryan who was having lunch with him. "And the little chickens."

"The Little Chickens like corn bread?" Bryan seemed surprised.

"They love it. The problem is that Taffy doesn't want me to give it to them."

Barney took the corn bread to the Little Chickens anyway, with Taffy following close behind him. She knew he had the corn bread in his pocket. The Little Chickens rushed up to the fence, their heads up, eyes fixed on Barney. They knew he had a treat for them, and they preferred the corn bread to the mixture of cracked grain and sunflower seeds that were their regular diet. Barney drew the little package from his pocket, crumbled some of the bread, and dropped the crumbs through the wire covering the pen. The Little Chickens rushed excitedly to pick up the crumbs. One young rooster grabbed the largest crumb, and ran with it in his beak. Two others chased him, demanding a share of the prize.

Rubbing the corn muffin on the wire covering, Barney reduced it to a shower of crumbs, falling into the chicken pen, where they were instantly picked up by the Little Chickens. Golden Boy, once the Fallen One and now the Cock of the Roost, picked up a large crumb, and clucked to the hens and the young ones. "Come and see!" he called. He wanted to share it with Pullet, for she was his favorite. She came eager, unaware of any danger. But danger was high overhead in the sky. Danger hovered for a moment on outspread wings, then dropped out of the sky, landing on the ground opposite Barney, stood against the fence, staring at the Little Chickens in the pen.

Barney was startled, but he made no sound. Inside his head he formed the words "A Chicken Hawk!" The Chicken Hawk was about two feet long from the tip of his curved yellow beak to the tip of his black and white tail feathers. Standing at the edge of the chicken pen, the Chicken Hawk closed his feathers silently and studied the Little Chickens. He did not see Barney, who formed the words inside his head again. "He's making a selection for his lunch!"

Moving the corn muffin gently over the wire, Barney kept the crumbs falling into the pen. The Little Chickens had not yet seen the hawk, whose yellow eyes were fixed on the flock. Light shades of white and dark grey blended into the landscape. He was motionless; Barney's hand ceased moving the corn bread, and the crumbs no longer fell into the pen. Then suddenly the Little Chickens were aware of the Chicken Hawk. They stopped picking up crumbs. Their heads went up in alarm, then turned to look into the eyes of the Chicken Hawk. They made sounds of alarm, but the Chicken Hawk remained motionless.

The mother hens, Little Grey Hen and Pullet, squawked loudly to alert their babies to the danger. Little Grey Hen ruffled the feathers on her neck; she extended her wings like two shields held by warriors. She rushed at the hawk, stopping only inches from the wire that separated them. He could have reached in and grabbed her, but the wire mesh was too tightly woven to permit this. Still, Little Grey Hen realized that she was in danger; she turned away from the unblinking yellow eyes and the curved beak, she turned and ran toward the open door of the hen house, herding her young ones inside, where she continued to emit sharp cries of alarm. Pullet came too with her little brood of three, and hurried inside. Golden Boy stood until hens and babies were all safe inside, then he too ran. He was Captain of the threatened ship, the last to enter the life boat. Barney stood motionless, but now the Chicken Hawk raised his staring yellow eyes, and looked into Barney's face.

He turned slightly to the right, lifted his great wings, and left the ground, his legs and talons hanging beneath him as he rose into the air. Barney watched, fascinated, wondering, as the great bird rose swiftly, silently into the sky, when he was high above the bean field, he screamed. Was it the scream of frustration? Or a warning that he would come back another day when the Little Chickens were not covered by the wire fence, or watched over by the man and the dog. For now Taffy made her presence known, ready to fight the intruder who had dared to enter her territory.

Barney breathed a sigh of relief, and turned to Taffy, who had now come right up beside him, still hoping to get some of the corn bread. "A good thing I didn't turn them out into the yard this morning. If they had been running loose, one of them would have been the Chicken Hawk's dinner now."

The Chicken Hawk was now history for Taffy. The corn bread was the item of the moment. Her eyes sparkled with excitement and expectation as she looked up at Barney. He gave the remaining corn bread to her. She accepted it gladly. Her body language said to him "Shucks! I would take on that ol' Chicken Hawk any day if I could just get at him. I'm not scared of any old Chicken Hawk."

"Yes, I know how brave you are. You would take on any thing, furred, feathered or finned. But it's still a good thing Bryan helped me put wire over the top of the chicken pen." Inside the chicken house the Little Chickens began to move about. Golden Boy came to the door, and looked out, then clucked to his flock. "Still alive," Barney said. "Safe."

Turning back to the house, Barney called to Taffy. "Come on, Old Girl. This calls for a cup of coffee for me. And that other corn muffin. You get it. Wouldn't be good for the Little Chickens to eat on a scared stomach."

Tale Fourteen: Decline
And Fall Of Golden Boy

Golden Boy emerged as the Cock of the Roost when Little Red was beaten by the coalition of Red and Golden cocks. But the place of supremacy in the hen yard is tenuous when there are as many cocks as hens.

Golden Boy stood proud, slender, with long curving tail feathers that touched the ground. His comb and wattles were red, his eyes bright. He strutted among the hens and the cocks. His golden plumage caught the rays of the sun and threw them back for all to see. He was a Prince among the cocks, admired by all the hens.

But on the evening before the big ice storm came, Barney was alerted by a loud squawking in the hen house. Sounds of alarm, distress, terror. Cries that pierced Barney deeply, sharply. Bringing from him an exclamation: "What the hell?" He rushed to the door of the hen house, flung it open and surprised two Reds making a quick exit into the hen yard. Looking guilty. On their faces and bodies was the expression of wrong doing. But a wrong unfinished. Before Barney's face they fled, reluctantly, looking back.

Barney stepped outside and went to the fence to count the chickens. Thinking: Now what have these two been up to? Then he noticed that Golden Boy was missing. But he distinctly remembered that Golden Boy had been in the hen house when he heard the racket. In the midst of the melee there. "Now what?" he said to Taffy who had rushed to the scene of battle, eager to get into the fight and put all of the chickens into the air.

Barney searched the hen house. He looked closely into the nests. He searched the corners and checked the roost poles. No Golden Boy. Could he have overlooked him in the hen yard? He went there again. No Golden Boy.

The Reds still had a criminal look about them. Barney was puzzled by it all.

Max the Manx cat had come now to investigate the goings on in the hen house. He bowed up his back at Taffy and made a pass at the chickens. "You stay back, Max." Barney scolded. "A chicken can't just disappear into a limited space. He was here. He didn't run out. No place for him to fly to. Golden Boy has to be here some place."

Barney sat down on the bale of wheat straw to contemplate the mystery. Something fluttered against his coat tail. He turned and looked into Golden Boy's frightened eyes. The eyes were all that he could see of Golden Boy. He was hiding in the wheat straw.

Barney reached to pick up Golden Boy but Golden Boy exploded in terror from his hiding place in the wheat straw. He flew wildly into the roof of the hen house, banged around up there a time or two, came to earth again and ran out into the hen yard. Darkness was coming on rapidly in advance of the ice storm and in the gloaming figures became indistinct when Barney got up from the bale of wheat straw and went again to look into the hen yard. Again, he could not see Golden Boy.

Taffy was yipping at the door, and Max was making mewing sounds of inquiry. Barney came back and searched the wheat straw again. This time he found Golden Boy buried deeper than before in the wheat straw. The two Reds were standing in the entrance, watching, ready to pounce, if they could find Golden Boy. Murder was in their eyes. Barney felt as if he had seen it in the eyes of his fellow men. What could be going on in this hen house become a mad house? Barney shut off the flashlight beam, went out and closed the door.

"I'll be damned," he said to Taffy and Max. "Well, when the morning breaks we will see who's crowing in this hen house."

Morning came, with a light skift of snow and some ice on the ground. Every branch and twig on the maple tree was encased in ice. The cocks in the hen house greeted the snowfall with raucous crowing. The Reds. Not Golden Boy. He was silent. Barney found him hiding in a nest. "Hey. Nests are for hens," Barney told him, and trapping Golden Boy with a fish net, he caught him and examined him closely. Golden Boy's once red comb was blackened by old blood where the Reds had pecked him. His eyes were filled with fear. He squawked when Barney took hold on him. Then he quieted down, watching to see what would happen to him in Barney's hands. Could it be worse than the Reds?

"I guess you will join Little Red in exile now," Barney said. "But then it may be a refuge. Depends on how you look at it. In any case, it will be one on one." He opened the door to the tool shed attached to the garage, and he set Golden Boy on the old discarded piano there. Golden Boy cackled in alarm as he looked about him at his new surroundings. At this new aspect of his fall from power.

"Now we will see," Barney said to Golden Boy, "if you and Little Red will fight it out for first place in the garage ... Or whether you will team up together." Morning came. Barney flung open the garage doors to get the car for his visit to the Sunrise Cafe. Little Red and Golden Boy were standing together, silently, with Little Hen standing nearby. A contented aspect covered Little Hen. Golden Boy had been accepted by both Little Red and Little Hen without a fight.

"Nursing your wounds, I guess," Barney said. "Both of you." The victorious Reds in the hen house were crowing lustily. "And you, celebrating your arrival at the top," he said to them. Neither Little Red nor Golden Boy was answering the Reds.

"Right," Barney said. "I reckon there's nothing to crow about in defeat." He turned to Taffy who was watching the little trio on the ground beside the old car. She yipped twice and looked into Barney's face.

Taffy's eyes were saying "They'll make it. Get the old car out and let's go to town. We're wasting time."

Tale Fifteen: Little Grey Hen Comes Visiting

On the morning of March Five Little Grey Hen dropped down from her perch on the old piano, and left her sanctuary in the garage where the antique car sat idle, and she came to visit Barney in the house.

First she ran out into the back yard under the old maple tree with the twisted bark. There she found the cracked corn and other small seeds Barney had put out earlier for the birds. She pecked at a few sunflower seeds. This was something entirely different for her, and she raised her shapely head, looking toward the house, saying "So this is what the wild birds get. Hmmm." Then, when she had tasted a little of everything, she turned her bright eyes toward the open door of the utility room. For Barney had left the door propped open because Max was on his early morning prowl, and he might decide at any moment that some danger lurked, and then he would make a wild dash for the safety of the house, and of Barney's physical presence.

Little Grey Hen hummed and sang her peculiar little song, thinking Now what is this? The open door was an invitation for her to explore. Without a moment's hesitation, she stepped boldly into the utility room and began her exploration. There was the bowl of Max's food, little star shaped pellets of dry and delicious tidbits. She pecked at it and scattered some of it onto the floor, but decided it was not better than sunflower seeds. Not too well impressed with cat food, Little Grey Hen leaped onto the sink which was filled with all sorts of junk, empty plastic buckets and black plastic dishes for frozen TV dinners, and corn cobs, and a few tiny specks of something.

She pecked at the tiny bits of food and two grains of corn, then turned to look at the fish tank. The water was green with algae, but the gold fishes were visible and Little Grey Hen wondered why they would live in water, studying them with her bright shining eye, but then she lost interest in them, for she had seen another open door.

This doorway led her, after she had hopped up a couple of steps, into the hallway filled with Barney's old boots and heavy socks, and brooms and mops and dust pans and cardboard boxes filled with she didn't know what, so she stood there studying it all, with neither approval nor disapproval, for she had never seen anything like this before, but soon she saw another open door; this one led to the bathroom.

In the bathroom she saw more strange things. There was a big tub that looked like a giant watering trough but all the water had run out of it. Up above, out of reach unless she decided to fly up there, was another bowl that looked like a smaller watering trough, but when she hopped up there, again, no water. On the floor again, she discovered water in a strangely shaped bowl, but when she tried to get to the water she soon saw that she could not reach it without falling in, so she turned away, and after pecking at a few Lady Bugs who had come in for the winter, she walked back out into the hallway. Now she faced another open doorway, and a new challenge, for before her bright and shining eyes, was the kitchen where Barney was cooking his breakfast. She stood transfixed with wonder at this miracle.

Still singing her strangely musical little song, and still wondering at the strange things she had seen in the bathroom, she now stood looking into the kitchen, and she would have marched right over to Barney who was standing over a fry pan of eggs on the stove. Barney felt a twinge of guilt about the eggs, but then his attention was shifted to a scene of conflict, for Taffy was lying across the entrance to the kitchen, and she did not intend to let Little Grey Hen enter this part of the house. Little Grey Hen sang her little song and eyed Taffy, then walked right past her into the kitchen.

Taffy growled and even yipped once, then looked at Barney for approval, but Little Grey Hen marched over to the stove and looked up. Barney covered the eggs with a skillet lid and put bread in the toaster. Then Little Grey Hen checked out the refrigerator and hopped up onto the kitchen sink and took a sip of water. It tasted of soap though because it was what Barney had used for washing up last night's dishes, so she shook her beak to fling the water off and hopped down onto the floor. Ignoring Taffy, she walked into the next area of the house and found herself facing Max.

Max was lying on Barney's desk in a very proprietary manner, and he was surprised to see Little Grey Hen. She was surprised to see him too and she thought: so this is where you stay when you are not out in the garage pestering me. Max had learned to pester from a safe distance because Little Grey Hen had pecked him once when he got too close. He had fled under the antique car and fixed his yellow eyes on her from a safe distance, and now he turned those yellow eyes on Little Grey Hen, but he did not dare challenge her right to be in the chair, which she had now mounted. Max had never solved the mystery of Little Grey

Hen, for when he visited the hen house where all the other chickens lived he sent them into a flutter and a flurry of cackling and flying about on the roost pole, but this Little Grey Hen was not at all afraid of him. She was boss in the garage and now she had extended her territory to the area where Barney lived and worked.

After close investigation of the typewriter on Barney's desk, she turned and left Max in charge there. She turned and went into the bedroom, and here was the strangest sight of all. Could it be possible that Barney actually slept on this bed? This called for a thorough investigation. She hopped up onto the bed and thought it might make a good nest in case she wanted to lay an egg, but it was really too big for that. Maybe a higher perch would give her a better perspective, so she hopped onto the head board. But Taffy had decided that this was going too far. She had followed Little Grey Hen into the bedroom and now she barked loudly at her. Barney came to see what was going on, for by now he had emptied the fry pan of eggs into a plate on the table. The toast had popped up too, but the ruckus in the bedroom demanded his attention.

When Barney reached the bedroom all was confusion because both Max and Taffy were challenging Little Grey Hen's right to be on the bed. This was, after all, their territory, for when Taffy was younger she would spring onto the bed and get close to Barney when the lightning and thunder and pounding rain came in the night. Now she was old and heavy and the bed seemed to be much higher off the floor, so she would come and whine for Barney to lift her up onto the bed. Once safe in his arms, she could turn a deaf ear to old Thunderer up there in the heavens. And now this Little Grey Hen was on the bed. The very idea! So she had called Barney to report this invasion of the bedroom.

But Little Grey Hen was not at all flustered by all this barking. No. She just marched out, clucking and singing her little song. She marched past Max who was bowing up in the back while he guarded the desk. Still singing her strange little song, Little Grey Hen marched out through the kitchen and the hallway and the utility room, with just a glance at the hot water heater, and out into the back yard to sample the sunflower seeds again.

Barney went back to his breakfast of eggs and bacon. The eggs were cold now but he ate them, remembering what had happened to Big Grey Hen and to Little Red and Golden Boy. Well, he sat wondering what had happened to them, for it was still a mystery. So he put a cap on his head and picked up his heavy stick which stood in the corner of the doorway. He called to Taffy and, said "We had better go out and check on things."

In the garage Barney found Little Grey Hen sitting on the lawn mower and surveying her domain with great domesticity. Then he went on to the hen house where his appearance caused all the hens and cocks to set up a furore of cackling, until they were reassured that it was just Barney and Taffy, and not a hawk or a coyote or a fox.

Taffy thought that such a silly display of excitement on the part of the chickens called for some reason, so she made a quick dash into the midst of them, barking and sending them all flying onto the roost pole.

"That reminds me," Barney said as he dumped cracked corn and wheat into the chickens' feed trough. "You haven't had your breakfast either. Come on Old Girl, back to the kitchen." Taffy came along and when they reached the doorway between the hall and the kitchen she lay down and took her position, to guard against any more invasions by feathered creatures.

But when the crowing and cackling had died down in the hen house, Barney could hear the soft musical notes of Little Grey Hen's song coming to him from the garage, for she had mounted the hood of the antique car and was happily examining her reflection in the windshield.

TALE SIXTEEN: MYSTERY OF THE MISSING CHICKENS

"They're gone!" Barney exclaimed as his blood pressure shot up and his face registered a mixture of anger and puzzlement. In the dark, of course, where nobody could see his face, if anybody had been there to see his face, and nobody was there except Taffy the little white dog.

He stared again, unbelieving, into the old barn of a hen house covered with rusty corrugated iron on the roof. The wooden door was standing open just as he had left it for the convenience of the retiring chickens, five hens and four roosters.

Now only two little banties were huddled together on the roost pole. A red and black and green rooster and a little brown and yellow hen. They cocked their beady little eyes at him when he threw the flashlight beam on them. "Should be nine of them here, not counting Little Red."

Thinking of Little Red, he walked quickly back to the garage, threw the beam of the flashlight through the window. Little Red crouched on the roof of the antique Plymouth. Barney had spread a canvas cover over the car's roof to protect it from Little Red's droppings. "Little Red's here," he said, speaking to the small, fat, shaggy white dog who peered up at him with bright black inquiring eyes filled with deep concern, for Taffy sensed that something was wrong here.

"That accounts for three," he added, doing the arithmetic for the little white dog's enlightenment. "But where are the other seven? Something's happened here. Those chickens should have gone in the hen house to roost."

A large dense Forsythia bush grew against the west wall of the hen house. Barney squatted beside the bush in darkness and shone a beam of light into the thick leafy branches and onto the ground under the bush. He saw nothing. "No chickens here," he told the little white dog who responded to his words by whining low and sad.

"If they were hiding under there they would be cackling and flapping about at sight of you." Taffy's appearance in the hen house was always enough to send the chickens into spasms of terror.

A big clump of tall privet bushes grew near the house on the South side. Barney squatted and peered inside the privet, swinging the beam of light all around. This produced the same result that the search of the Forsythia bush had done. No roosting chickens. "This is getting serious now," he remarked. Taffy responded with a small yip which he interpreted to mean "Very serious."

Barney and Taffy went inside the house to regroup. He spoke to the yellow tailless Manx cat named Max. "I was gone no more than forty minutes and seven chickens have disappeared into the darkness ... No, Max, I do not need your help. I had enough trouble getting you into the house before I left. If I hadn't wasted so much time with you I would have been back here before dark and I could have herded the chickens into the house the way I always do."

He sat down to contemplate the situation and Max leaped onto his lap, stretched out on his legs and promptly fell asleep, feeling no guilt about the chickens. On sunshiny days Max gained great pleasure from staring at the chickens until they became nervous and began to run and cackle, but when they turned on him he would run up the big maple tree and crouch in the lower fork of it, staring at the chickens until they lost their nerve, began to cackle hysterically and ran away. Now Barney threw the flashlight beam up into the branches of the maple tree because earlier in the afternoon he had seen some of the little cocks flying down from the tree amid much crowing and cackling. He saw no chickens in the maple tree.

"I'll look on the roof of the hen house," he said to Taffy who had followed outside again. The beam of light swept across the rusty corrugated iron roof, revealing no roosting chickens. He did the same for the garage and the adjoining tool shed, looking again in the window at Little Red crouched on the roof of the old car. Same result. No chickens.

Back inside the house, he closed up both the dog and the cat, and returned to the search. This time for feathers. "If some animal has caught them there should be feathers scattered about. But what animal would catch seven chickens and carry them off?" Finding no feathers, he added "and not leave a feather."

He searched the narrow band of tall grass that bordered the lawn and the adjacent bean field. The beans had been harvested and there was no cover out there to conceal a sparrow, let alone seven chickens. Barney was not one to give up easily; he made three more circuits of the yard, shining his flashlight into every corner, crack and crevice. Then he gave up and went inside to fret and worry and wonder.

He tried to read. The book was Ben Ames Williams'
Leave Her to Heaven but he could not concentrate, and
found himself reading the same paragraph twice. A friend
knocked on the door and came in. Barney told him about
the disappearance of the chickens. "Where could they be?"
he asked his friend. "Somebody must have come here while
I was gone and lifted them off the roost, stuffed them in a
sack and made his getaway before I got back."

"I didn't do it," his friend said, "But why would anybody
steal those little runty things when the country is dotted
with chicken houses full of chickens just waiting to go into
the pot?" Joe thought about it some more and said "Unless
it was a Halloween prank, he must be crazy."

"I'd make him crazy if I could catch him in that hen house,"
Barney told his friend who laughed nervously because he
wondered if Barney thought he had got the chickens, and
pretty soon Joe said he had to go home and get some sleep
because he had to go to work in the morning.

After a long time Barney went to bed because his eyes
were stinging and after another long time he fell asleep
and dreamed about counting chickens and in the dream he
kept saying "They don't add up to ten." When he awakened
it was daylight and he went to the window and looked out.
He could see shadowy shapes moving about in front of the
chicken house and picking at the grass by the closed door.
He went out, opened the door to the hen house and said
"Chick Chick Come Chick Chick." They all ran inside the
hen house and hurried over to the feed pan.

Later that day Barney's friend Joe came again and asked
about the chickens. Barney said "He brought them back."
Joe stared at him and Barney said "the chicken thief. He
brought them back just before daylight. Didn't make any
noise either or I would have waked up and seen him."

"Beats me," Barney's friend. Joe said. "Wonder where those crazy chickens were hiding. Chickens are funny, you know, about where they'll roost at night. Now you take Little Red..."

TALE SEVENTEEN: VARMINT PROOF?

The weather turned cool in late September, and this reminded Barney that he would have to do something about the hen house. It was unusual for the nights to be so cool so early, but everything about the little chickens seemed unusual to Barney. There they were, high in the maple trees, safe from attack by night travelers who had not the ability to climb up into the big trees and climb out onto a small tree limb, and pluck a chicken off it. But the maple trees were clothed in a thick green foliage now; what would happen when the leaves turned yellow and red and orange and brown, and then came drifting down to the ground, leaving the branches bare?

Barney would be raking and loading the leaves into the wheelbarrow and hauling them to the edge of the corn field, or maybe he would be smart enough to wait for a strong wind to blow them off the lawn. But in any case, the branches of the trees would be bare, then they would be coated with snow and ice and freezing rain. What then, Little Chickens? Will you be happy up there then?

Or will you go looking again at the hen house? Will you have forgotten those two terrible nights when the opossum came and killed your mates and terrorized you? Will you remember only that the hen house is snug and dry and warm because the snow and freezing rain and blowing wind won't penetrate it, and you can sleep comfortably on the roost poles I have put there for that purpose?

Barney thought about all these things and he said to the little chickens who were picking in the litter under the maple trees "If that is possible, had I not better get to work on that hen house and make it varmint proof? And since I am not a carpenter, what about somebody to help me? Who will that be?"

Taffy came and looked up into Barney's face. Taffy's black eyes were trying to tell him something and finally he got the message. "Brian, of course. Brian will help me." Barney looked at the gaping hole where the possum had entered, and he said "Brian is just the man for this job. He is handy with tools and he will know how to do it." This seemed to please Taffy, and Barney went on thinking out loud. "That opening is way up near the roof, between the roof and the boards which form the sides of the structure. It would be hard to reach up there and work while standing on the ground, and that ladder, well, I don't trust it."

Taffy's bright black eyes seemed to validate what Barney had said about the folly of climbing that rickety step ladder with the first step missing. "Yes, you are right about that ladder, Old Girl. It's all I can do to keep my balance on level ground. If I climb that ladder … Well, that's settled then. I'll call Brian." So that is just what Barney did, and Brian wanted to know if he had the necessary materials. They agreed that they would need some boards and nails and a hammer and a saw, and the ladder, of course. But mainly what Barney needed was Brian who was young and agile and strong and … and a carpenter.

So Brian came and they drove in his pickup truck to the building supply place downtown and loaded the boards, three of them, one by six inches and ten feet long, because

Brian had brought a tape measure and they had determined just how long the boards would have to be. Then they sawed them into pieces that would fit into all the openings under the roof, and Brian nailed them up while Barney and Taffy and Max and the four little chickens stood by watching Brian. They stapled the wire up to close the openings completely and stood back to look at the work they had done.

"Varmint proof." Barney pronounced it when he had measured the cracks between the boards with his eyes. "Nothing can get in there now but a black snake, and the snakes will be in their winter dens. Let's go and have a cup of coffee." So Barney and Brian went to the house for coffee and they watched out the back window to see what the little chickens would do. The little chickens, full of curiosity, walked over and looked inside. They even poked their heads and necks inside and looked all around. Little Red Rooster led the way, and they went inside. Little Grey Hen followed Little Red Rooster. Then Pullet and the Fallen One came on inside. They looked at the work Barney and Brian had done, then they walked back outside, turned their backs on the hen house, and ran to the big privet bush where they stood around in the shade and did not look again at the hen house.

Brian read the disappointment in Barney's face. He said "You just wait until cold weather. When winter comes with snow and ice and blasting wind, they'll change their minds. YOU just wait."

Brian went home, leaving Barney to study his situation some more. This is just what he did too. "I'll leave the door open," he said to Taffy. And he propped the door open with a flat rock. He examined the black plastic buckets for nests and put fresh straw in them. He kicked the straw and litter on the floor. He touched the roost poles to be certain that they were strong and stable. Again he pronounced the hen house "Varmint proof. But maybe it's chicken proof too because the fear is still in their heads." Taffy's bright black eyes said "I'll just have a look around." She went inside and sniffed about until she was fully satisfied, then her eyes spoke to Barney. "Everything is okay except the chickens. They just need a little coaxing to get them to go in where they belong."

Taffy dashed away to the privet bush where the little chickens were dusting themselves, and she charged under the privet bush, barking with great fervor. The chickens left their dust baths on the ground and took cover in the upper branches of the privet bush where they cackled and set up a great noise and excitement. Two of them even ran out of the privet bush and flew up into the big maple tree in the back yard, looking back at this white terror that had come upon them while they were having their dust baths.

"I don't think that will work, Taffy," Barney said. "You come with me. We'll have to try something else." Barney scooped up some scratch feed and put it inside the chicken house. He poured water into a plastic pan and set it on the floor inside. Propping the door open wide, he said "Now we will see what happens." And looking up into the sky which was beginning to cloud up, he added, "And we will see what help we get from above."

TALE EIGHTEEN: A GREY CHICKEN TALE

This is the tale of Little Grey Boy, a lovesick rooster.

Little Grey Boy was the third bantam cock introduced to the hen yard. Mostly white, with some black feathers in his wings, Little Grey Boy came with his own mate, a little grey hen who stayed faithfully by his side, even after he had been whipped soundly by Little Red.

Little Grey Boy's high upstanding red comb and prominent wattles and his handsome curving tail feathers made an impressive appearance, and his long sharp spurs equipped him well for battle, but Little Red had already shown himself the cock of the hen yard by trouncing Golden Boy who came before Little Grey Boy. Golden Boy suffered ignominious defeat and humiliation because Little Red was seething with resentment at Big Red, a tremendous Rhode Island Red rooster who dominated the hen yard with heavy beak and feet.

So when Big Red disappeared mysteriously one day – Barney traded Big Red downriver because of his heavy footed behavior in beating up on everybody in the pen – Little Red became the Cock of the Roost. Little Grey Boy accepted his low place on the pecking order, and was content with his loyal wife, but one day Little Grey Hen became sick and died, leaving Little Grey Boy lonely and frustrated.

Little Grey Boy mourned his loss for all of three days, then he discovered the Big Grey Hens, Numbers One and Two, who were now on the mating market since the disappearance of Big Red. Little Grey Boy now ran hopefully, solicitously with the two Big Grey Hens as they chased after bugs and emerging cicadas and other choice tidbits in the lawn. The Big Grey Hens welcomed Little Grey Boy's company and even seemed to appreciate his help in finding bugs, cicadas and microscopic tidbits in the lawn. He would scratch his wing with his foot to let them know of intentions which he was never bold enough to carry out. Little Grey Boy clucked to the Big Grey Hens to announce his discovery of a fat cicada just emerging from underground and ready to climb up on the trunk of a maple tree, dry its wings and fly away to some love tryst of its own. But that ambition was never realized because Little Grey Boy found the emerging cicada and called the Big Grey hens who came running to the feast.

Little Grey Boy was both proud and happy when they accepted his offering; he had forgotten Little Grey Hen and her unswerving loyalty to him. He was now running with the Big Girls. Then Big Grey Hen Number One became broody, as the female of the species· is apt to do at a certain point in the cycle, for she was only answering the call of Nature, and she took her place on the last two eggs laid in the bucket nest. She now exhibited a belligerent and possessive attitude toward all intruders. She even pecked Barney sharply and ruffled her neck feathers and complained in the manner of old setting hens when he attempted to remove the two eggs for his breakfast. Barney was not a man to fight against Mother Nature, so he set up another plastic bucket nest in another corner of the hen house in the hope that Big Grey Hen Number Two and the little mates of the Red and Golden cocks would lay eggs in this alternate nest and he would not suffer deprivation in his normal breakfast menu.

But then Big Grey Hen Number Two became broody too and she squeezed into the nest with Number One. They quarreled over space because it was a tight fit, but eventually they achieved a sisterly sharing of the bucket nest, and Little Grey Boy settled onto the roost pole near the nest to watch over his two new wives who had gone to this advanced phase of the process without once allowing him to actually mate with them.

Some actions are contagious – at least that was Barney's appraisal of matters in the hen nest when Little Brown Hen edged her way into the nest and settled down between the two big hens. Little Grey Boy moved even closer to the bucket nest and watched over this strange nesting/brooding operation. He clucked and encouraged the three hens to produce some offspring but they were so crowded that they pushed the two eggs out onto the floor and the eggs were broken.

This over crowded arrangement lasted for four days. First the Little Brown Hen gave up in frustration, or despair, or disgust. Then Big Grey Hen Number Two decided not to hatch nonexistent eggs.

Then the original brooder, Big Grey Hen Number One, flounced off the nest, quarreling querulously with all observers and did not return. She ran with wildly flapping wings to the shaded area under the maple trees in the back yard and renewed her search for grubs, bugs and cicadas. After this turn of events, something that Barney never expected to see in his whole life time happened. Little Grey Boy took his place in the empty nest and began brooding.

The writer of this strange chicken tale wishes he could tell the expectant reader that Little Grey Boy laid an egg and hatched it, for that would be one for the Ripley Museum. But alas, Little Grey Boy came to a tragic end. His brooding activity caused the other roosters: both Red and Golden, to consider him a misfit, and they excluded him from their company. He became a loner; he strayed farther and farther from the flock, even becoming a daytime companion with Little Red who had already been exiled by the Red/Golden Coalition. Little Grey Boy now returned late in the evening to the roost in the hen house. Later and later, until one evening darkness came and Little Grey Boy had not come to roost. Barney closed the door, saying "I wonder where Little Grey Boy is, but I can't leave the house open. A predator may..."

That night a predator did come. The Death Angel found Little Grey Boy, huddled in the tall grass by the South wall of the hen house, and when morning light brought Barney in response to the concerted songs of the Golden and Red cocks in the hen house, he found the grey feathers scattered in the grass

Tale Nineteen: Little Grey Hen Has A New Baby

"**H**ey! Look at this!" Barney called to Taffy who stood expectantly watching at the hen house door. "An egg! Little Grey Hen is laying again!"

This was news. For there had been no eggs since Little Grey Hen and Pullet had hatched their broods of five and three, and had concentrated all their energies on protecting the young chicks and teaching them to eat, plus all the tricks of survival in the hen yard.

Now Little Grey Hen's chicks, two roosters and three pullets, had grown up. The roosters, one red and one buff colored, had grown long curving tail feathers and tall red combs standing on their heads; they were almost as tall as the Big Boy, but not quite ready to challenge his authority.

"It won't be long though," Barney predicted when he heard the cacophony of calls from the crowing roosters at sunup each morning. And the three pullets stood around watching, like teenage girls waiting for an invitation to their first prom. Little Grey Hen was tired of having them trailing her everywhere, and she gave them a peck or two to let them know she had other things to do. "Go about your own business now and don't expect me to show you where all the goodies are."

"And now," Barney said, rubbing his chin with one hand and holding to the roost pole with the other, "here's the reason. Little Grey Hen is ready to start a whole new family, and here's the first egg toward that end."

So Barney watched the nest in the black plastic bucket in the corner of the hen roost. Each day a new egg appeared in that nest, and he counted eight eggs, then Little Grey Hen began to show signs of wanting to brood again. She ran about with feathers and wings fluffed out, clucking in a quarrelsome manner, and avoided the other members of the flock. Then she settled into the nest, still quarreling when Barney drew near.

"Wait a minute! Hold on here!" Barney exclaimed "Winter time is coming soon. And I'm not sure I want to carry a whole new brood of baby chicks through the winter."

But Little Grey Hen was determined to sit on those eggs and hatch out a whole new brood of chicks, and Barney was determined to avoid that if possible, so he came up with a compromise. He lifted all the eggs but one, with Little Grey Hen quarreling and pecking him every time he took out an egg. Then he put in one store bought egg from WalMart, so Little Grey Hen now had two eggs. "One of them will hatch," he told her, "and the other one will make you feel better about it."

Then Barney waited and waited and waited because Little Grey Hen sat and sat and sat. For twenty one days. And on the twenty first day, Barney went to the hen house early in the morning, as the sun was coming up over the bean field. Little Grey Hen was down on the floor, clucking and calling, and in the nest Barney found one little chick, calling to its Mama to help him down from that bucket nest so high off the ground.

The chick was a little bundle of yellow fuzz about the size of two thimbles. "Oho! Little Yellow Puffball! I reckon you need some help." So Barney closed his hand around the little chick and set him on the floor beside his Mama who showed her appreciation for Barney's help by flying at him and pecking his hand. "Maternal Love!" Barney commented, rubbing the red spot on his hand.

All the other chickens in the hen house stood on the roost pole and gazed on this miracle in wonder and admiration. And Barney's friend Bryan came and saw the hen and biddy on the floor. He said "But won't the big chickens trample that little fellow?" Because the Little Yellow Puffball appeared to be so small and vulnerable among the other Little Chickens who appeared to be giants now by comparison.

"Oh no! Just Watch!" And whenever one of the other chickens came close Little Grey Hen fluffed out her feathers and spread her wings and made threatening sounds, so that the other chicken stood apart in fear. But in reality, the other chickens were not going to hurt the baby chick. "Just look and see how they all want to mother that chick as if it were their very own." And indeed they did. For animals love babies, and Little Chickens are animals with wings and feathers.

Barney turned to Taffy. "We have an even dozen now. That's enough! Enough for our limited space. What will we do if Pullet wants to brood too?"

"Well," Taffy's face said to Barney's understanding mind, "Little Yellow" – for now the Puffball had been dropped from his name – "Little Yellow doesn't take up much space. Maybe one more..."

"We will see then. Maybe a baker's dozen could fit in there ... if I put up another roost pole."

TALE TWENTY: A
MYSTERY IS SOLVED

B arney saw his neighbor Jim working at the end of his driveway. Snapping Taffy's leash onto her collar, he walked down to visit. After he had satisfied his curiosity about what Jim was doing – he was widening his driveway – Barney managed to turn the conversation to his chickens, for he could not get rid of the idea that somehow those chickens had disappeared in the direction of Jim's place. So when Jim commented on the fence Barney had built, Barney said "It's a chicken pen in reverse. A fence around my garden to keep the chickens out."

Jim paused in the work he was doing – trying to lift a heavy block of concrete out of the way of the construction job on the driveway – wiped some sweat from his face, and said "I saw some chickens in the woods back there." He waved his arm in the direction of the large wooded area behind his house. "Chickens or guineas, or something. I know you once said something about your guineas flying over here."

"Right. Where do you say you saw these chickens?"

"In the woods behind my barn."

"Hmmm. Wonder how they got there. How long ago was this ?"

"It's been about two weeks now since I saw them. Two of them."

Barney's two little cocks, Little Red and Golden Boy had been gone for two months, but memory can be fuzzy where time is concerned.

"Wish you'd called me." Barney said, looking at Jim's big black dog who was trying to court Taffy, who wasn't having any of it.

"Old Blackie there will catch them and eat them if he can." Jim seemed proud of Blackie's skill at catching squirrels or anything else that moves and breathes and runs upon the earth. "He tries to catch the deer when they cross the field. Almost caught one too."

Barney said "I'll search the woods for the missing cocks." But when he thought about how big the woods were, he turned to his friend Joe for help. "A search and find rescue mission," he told Joe. "Let's walk those woods and see if the little cocks are there. We've had a lot of snow since they disappeared, and they might have starved by now if they are in there."

"Wild birds survive," Joe said, trying to be encouraging.

"Yes. Some do. The ones who come to my feeder in the back yard. But these little fellows? ... I've never even heard the sound of crowing in these woods."

Barney and Joe and Taffy set out upon their search for the missing cocks though. "How will you catch them if you find them out here in the woods?" Joe asked.

"Don't know. Have to build a trap for them, I guess."

"I know how to make a trap. But we have to find the chickens first. No use to make a trap if the chickens are not here."

Finding two little chickens in a big woods proved to be a daunting task. Barney and Joe separated and walked forty yards apart to cover more territory. Taffy stayed close to Barney in the dense woodland, but then they came to a deep ditch. She tried to climb the bank, but failed, turned back, and headed toward home. Barney was struggling and puffing too. He decided to follow Taffy. There were more ditches with water in them, intersecting the woods, and they came to an old abandoned refrigerator. Taffy sniffed, squatted, and peed on it, then scratched leaves. "No chicken here, I guess." Barney was amused at Taffy's action. They had passed a pond as they entered the woods. Now Taffy wanted to investigate it. They were welcomed by the sound of frogs who had discovered Spring had come. Taffy tried to catch a frog, he jumped, splashing water on her; she shook the water onto Barney, and went hunting for another adventure. This was much better than climbing out of deep ditches.

Barney called to Joe and said "Taffy thinks we have gone far enough. She's walked about enough."

Joe was checking for chicken droppings among the leaves, and for any evidence of scratching among the leaves. "Nothing but bird lime," he said in disgust. Barney sighted a hawk sailing overhead. "Bet there's the fellow who got my roosters." Then he found a patch of rabbit fur in the leaves. "Here's where he made his lunch one day." But the bird lime and the rabbit fur were all the signs they saw.

They came back to Jim's barn and Barney said "Let's check out the barn. Those cocks wouldn't roost in a tree if there's a barn handy." Searching through more old rusty cars and junk, the two men and a dog did not even turn up one bit of chicken droppings. "Can't understand it. Big snow. They would come to the barn." But no luck. All three of them trudged home, dispirited. As soon as they opened the door, Taffy flopped on the kitchen floor and was soon snoring.

The cocks in the hen house started crowing, and the little cock who had replaced Little Red and Golden Boy as the new husband for Little Grey Hen, began answering their challenge.

"Sunday morning antiphonal choir," Barney chuckled. "I don't believe they even miss Little Red and Golden Boy."

"Maybe they do and that's what they are singing about. Can you interpret chicken language?"

Barney poured coffee for Joe and himself, then sat down. Max came and hopped onto his knees. Taffy raised her head, having shaken off the nap, turned a baleful glance at Max. She barked at the cat. Barney said "I can tell you what she's saying."

Joe grinned as he sipped his coffee. "What did she say?"

"She said "Get off his lap, you lazy, good for nothing cat. You didn't even go with us to hunt the chickens and now, you want it all."

Next day: A surprising event occurred; it changed the picture. Barney had been to town. Joe had come, and Taffy was on her leash, tied to the front porch post, barking to let Joe know of the invasion. Joe looked out across the old bean field and saw Old Blackie running with something in his mouth. He yelled at the dog who increased his pace, running for home. Jim came out on his tractor and yelled at Blackie. Blackie opened his mouth and the little Red and Black Cock hit the ground running. Blackie ran after him and Jim ran after Blackie and Joe ran after them all, and Barney arrived and ran after the whole pack.

The little cock saw the open barn door and he ran for it. Inside the barn he found the perfect hiding place. A thousand perfect hiding places. Old rusted out auto frames, big boxes, old mattresses, piles of lumber, an indescribable collection of junk. The little cock ran under for cover.

Jim now turned to Old Blackie. Blackie tried to run but Jim nabbed him and hooked a great long chain on him. Blackie still wanted the chicken who hid himself, terrified under the junk and plunder that had gathered there in the barn for forty years. "He ran in there," Jim said, panting. He was dragging the long heavy chain and holding to Blackie's collar. "He's in the barn. Maybe we can catch him." He snapped the chain onto Blackie's collar and came to help.

Barney saw the little rooster hovering inside a box but when he tried to catch him he ran out through a hole in the box.

Jim said "I got close to him out there in the bean field but couldn't catch him. Boy, he can run."

"But not fast enough to get away from Old Blackie," Barney said, stumbling over the junk in the barn. The little rooster looked out at him from under a great pile of rubbish. They closed the barn door.

Joe looked on helpfully. "Too many hiding places under all this junk. You'll have to wait."

"Wait for what?"

"Wait for night. He will fly up and roost on top of all this junk and you can catch him then."

They put scratch feed and a little pan of water on the ground near an old open refrigerator box. "I'll come back tonight." Barney and Joe turned away. Jim glared again at Old Blackie and said "I'll have to get a heavier chain."

"He's scared now," Barney said, "and with good reason." His gaze swept over all the high places where the chicken might want to roost. He and Joe and Taffy went back to the house to wait for night, but he could not remember ever wanting night to come on. And when it did, it came with a rain storm, with lightning and thunder and rain pelting on the roof of Jim's sky lighted barn. Still, Barney went with flashlight and fish net, and stumbling over all the junk, throwing his beam all about, there seemed to be nothing but junk everywhere in the darkness. He was about to give up when the light glanced off the bright feathers hovering on a shelf high above the old boxes and the litter of years of throw away collection. He held the beam steady and the little cock's eyes reflected the light; creeping closer, Barney slipped the fish net over him, but when he reached for the cock, he squirmed out and flew away to another high perch.

Barney waited for him to settle himself again, dropped the fish net and held onto the flashlight. He threw the beam into the little cock's eyes. Paralyzed by the light and by fear, the bird sat still for a moment, and Barney closed his hands over him. He struggled. His sharp spurs dug into Barney's wrists, but Barney held on, hugged him to his chest. Somehow he managed the flashlight and the fish net and the barn door, and the pelting rain, until he reached the car, then climbed in, and driving with one hand, he made it home.

"Now." Barney carried the little cock to the tool shed on the back of the garage. He opened the door and shone the light onto the old piano. There sat Little Grey Hen. He set the rooster beside the thrice widowed Little Grey Hen; she sang her strange little song. The little cock ruffled his feathers, smoothed them down, and settled beside her for sleep.

At dawn he crowed triumphantly, even before the cocks in the hen house made their announcement of the new day.

TALE TWENTY ONE: TWELFTH

Twelfth was born out of season. Late. Baby chickens should be born in the Spring of the year. Not late Fall. But it had been an unusual year. Cool all Summer and warm in the Fall, Little Grey Hen had already raised the early flock. Five. Two cockerels and three pullets. All born in June. On the very day Barney came home from the hospital. And his friend Nancy had brought them into the utility room, creating a problem there because when Pullet's three were born, they had to share the utility room, and Little Grey Hen and Pullet were quarrelsome.

But Little Grey Hen had performed her duties, raising the two cockerels and three pullets. The young cockerels had begun to crow in rasping voices, challenging Big Red's supremacy. Big Red was the new name for The Fallen One who had Risen Again. Now the young cocks were trying to mount the pullets who stood around like teenage girls waiting to be invited to the prom. But when the young cocks leaped onto their backs, the pullets squawked desperately. "Oh No! I'm not ready for that!"

Twelfth though. Barney had not planned for Twelfth. He had not planned for Little Grey Hen to brood again. But the weather was unseasonably warm. And Mother Nature signalled. Little Grey Hen responded. She was to brood again. She had a small clutch of eggs, and her intent was unmistakable, so Barney said "Okay. You win. But only ONE EGG. Winter is coming, But I guess we can take care of ONE CHICK, since you are determined to have it this way."

Little Grey Hen settled onto her ONE EGG, pecked Barney's hand to let him know that he had better not try to take it away from her. And there she sat on that ONE EGG in the black plastic bucket lodged in between the roost poles. There she sat for twenty one days. She came off for food and water three times, returning all fluffed up and quarrelsome each time before the ONE EGG COULD GET COLD.

And on the twenty first day a tiny yellow chick, with small brown stripes on its wings emerged from that EGG. It was a MIRACLE!

Barney discovered this MIRACLE at sunrise on the twenty first day, when he opened the creaky door to the old hen house, and peered inside. For Little Grey Hen was standing on the floor, clucking urgently for the new born chick to descend from the bucket nest lodged between the roost poles four feet above the floor. And the tiny new born chick was cheeping desperately for Little Grey Hen to provide the needed help to make that descent. And sitting on the roost poles were ten Little Chickens, five cocks and five hens, waiting and watching to see what would happen next. For they knew that a MIRACLE had occurred, but they did not know how that Miracle was going to get its feet on the ground, nor how it would affect their lives.

Barney stood looking at all of this, and he said "Well!" And he took the tiny yellow chick with a brown streak running along each wing, and he set it on the floor beside Little Grey Hen, who flew at him and pecked him furiously because he had dared to touch her Baby.

Barney rubbed the red spot on his hand where Little Grey Hen had pecked him, and he stood contemplating his MIRACLE. He said "What shall I call it? I don't even know whether it is male or female. Will it grow to be another cock, and add his voice to the chorus that greets the sunrise every morning? Or will it be another hen, laying eggs and brooding more babies? If a cock, then I will have six cocks and six hens. If a hen, then an imbalance. Seven hens and five cocks." He counted the Little Chickens staring at him from the roost poles. "What shall I call it while I wait to see what it will be?"

Taffy nudged him with her cold nose and woofed at him. Her black eyes told him "Twelfth!"

So Twelfth was born more than twelve days before Christmas, and it seemed to Barney that Twelfth was so small running about underfoot among the big Little Chickens that he might get trampled. Indeed, Barney's special friend who had helped when Little Grey Hen's first batch was born, said "Won't they trample and peck the little thing to death?"

But at that moment Little Grey Hen flew into the biggest of the young cocks, and pecked him soundly, then turned on a pullet who was standing innocently by and watching. Barney answered his friend's concern. "I guess Little Grey Hen will take care of her MIRACLE with a vengeance fitting primal motherhood."

So with Little Grey Hen pecking and flogging all the others in the pen, Twelfth moved under that protective umbrella into the chicken pen and grew like Topsy, as if having arrived late he must hurry to the goal of Roosterdom or Hendom, and Barney is still unsure, which. He remarked to Taffy when the Deep Freeze of Christmas had passed.

"If he's a Cock, he's the only one who didn't get his comb frost bitten when the temp dropped to zero."

"How" Taffy's black eyes responded. "With his head tucked under Little Grey Hen's protective wing, how could he get his comb frost bitten?!"

Tale Twenty Two: Little Red Meets The Lion

"The Lion is coming," Barney announced to Taffy and Max. "His parents are bringing Leo at Thanksgiving. Get ready."

Leo, Barney's then one and only grandson, one and one half years old and precocious, came, and neither Taffy nor Max knew what to make of this unprecedented event. Leo himself came with high expectations because his MaMa and his DaDa had built up a full head of steam about the visit to Grampa's house at Thanksgiving. Leo was immediately attracted to Taffy and he ran to her in full expectation of being received with equal happiness. She growled when Leo took hold upon her ears and explored her eyes with his little fingers. Barney tried to explain to Taffy that little boys have a lot of curiosity about the eyes and ears with which dogs come equipped.

Max did not permit Leo to come into physical contact with him. He stared with big green round eyes at Leo, and when he had sized up the situation he fled, hid behind the aquarium in the utility room and watched Leo to see what move he would make next. Leo lost interest in both Taffy and Max; he moved on to the chicken pen where both cocks and hens stared at him in wonder and alarm and cackled anxiously in the expectation that he might break through the wire fence that he was leaning on and shaking vigorously.

Leo looked up at his MaMa and his DaDa and smiled because he was very pleased by all these colorful and exciting chickens. He even looked up at his Grampa, radiating his great pleasure. The chickens also stared at Barney and seemed to be saying "Now what is this all about?"

Barney was proud to show off the red and Golden cocks and the little Brown and yellow and grey hens who stared back at Barney's grandson. But there was more to see. "Little Red," Barney said. "Let's go and see Little Red. I'll bet he is just waiting with bated breath to meet my grandson."

Little Red was waiting. His hackles rose at sight of Leo. That is, the feathers on his neck rose and he prepared for flight, for Grandson Leo was moving rapidly toward Little Red and Little Hen. Leo's precocity was most evident in his motor skills. He had not decided which of the two chickens he would catch first. Maybe both of them. But he did not catch either of them. Little Hen flew into the garage window and beat her wings wildly against the glass. Little Red flew onto the roof of the old car, but feeling that his homeland was not secure there, he flew into the other window and beat his wings against it. Both Little Red and Little Hen seemed to think that if they beat their wings against the window it would open and let them escape from Leo.

The window did not open and the exuberant boy closed on them, laughing joyously at the prospect of coming into contact with the chickens. The window glass held firmly, and both Little Red and Little Hen gave up on it and flew down, knocking over a hammer, a screw driver, a can of nails and a sickle from the shelf where Barney had piled them so that they would be handy whenever he needed them.

Being on the ground again heightened the peril of Little Red and Little Hen. They cackled wildly and flew into the wall, fell back to the ground and ran under the old car. There they cackled in dire distress until Barney coaxed Leo to come with him, promising him something even more exciting than the chickens, although he had not yet thought about what that might be. It was Max. While Barney was closing the garage doors Leo found Max who had come to see what had excited the chickens more effectively even than he could do. Leo immediately forgot the chickens and ran to Max, fully confident that Max would be as happy to see him as he was to see Max. Leo attempted to take Max up in his arms in an affectionate hug, but Max was not happy at the prospect of being hugged by Leo.

Max sputtered briefly, then ran to the big Maple tree with the bark that twists artistically about its trunk. He climbed the tree until he was well beyond Leo's reach. Then he stopped climbing and looked down in terror, his yellow eyes big and round. The boy was gleefully cheering him on from the ground at the base of the tree. Leo wanted Max to climb even higher but Max knew that he was safe, so he crouched in a crotch of the tree and studied the boy on the ground.

Little Red uttered a strangled, hoarse, shrill sound that could be called a rooster crowing. It might have only been an expression of gratitude that he had been delivered from the clutches of the Lionhearted Boy. It might have been a warning to Max to stay as high in the tree as he could get. Taffy and all the other grownups were happy about the performance; Barney's grandson Leo was the happiest of all. What a Thanksgiving.

TALE TWENTY THREE:
THE GAY COCKS

B arney sat at the picnic table in the shade of the Maple trees in the back yard. The table was made of old cedar boards with moss growing on them. The boards were the remnants of the house that had burned. Everything had burned except the steps to the deck and Barney had salvaged the boards and built the table and benches. Now Barney relaxed in the shade; the temperature had reached ninety, and the shade was a life saver for both Barney and the Little Chickens.

The Little Chickens were bunched up in the shade, clucking and making little chicken sounds that indicated they could easily get very excited about a shadow that passed over. Barney counted them, and remarked to Taffy. "Two missing. Cocks. Twelfth and Ajax. Where could they be?" Taffy showed a total lack of interest in the whereabouts of Twelfth and Ajax. She lay stretched in the grass under the Maple trees. Then Barney heard familiar sounds corning from the hen house. Cackling.

But what would Ajax and Twelfth be cackling about? He laid his book aside, rose from the moss covered table, and walked quietly toward the hen house. Now the cackling increased. Crowing too. Barney eased into the doorway and peered inside. His eyes had to accommodate to the semi-darkness. Then he saw them. Twelfth was in the black plastic bucket nest. He was clucking and cackling and scratching about in the nest. Ajax was standing on the rim of the bucket. He was clucking and cackling and crowing.

When the two became aware of Barney's presence in the open doorway, they became quiet for a moment, staring at Barney. Then they cackled in great excitement and seemed to be very self conscious. "What are you two roosters doing on a nest?" Barney said in amazement. The two cocks, Twelfth and Ajax stared back at Barney. What was the expression in their eyes? Had they been caught in something? They cackled loudly. Guiltily?

Barney closed the door, walked back to the table in the shade, and looked again at Taffy. "Gay Cocks! I do believe Twelfth was trying to lay an egg, and Ajax was offering encouragement, telling him how to do it. Now what do you think of that, Taffy?"

Taffy spoke eloquently in body language as she rolled in the grass, rubbing her back against the ground. "Chickens," she said. "What do you expect from a couple of chickens? Just roosters being roosters."

Tale Twenty Four: A
New Champion

March came in like a lion with bad breath. Cold, windy. But the sun was shining. And the Little Chickens in their little house were eager to get out and flap their wings. When Barney cracked the door open and peered in, they rushed past him, cackling with anticipation of freedom. Eager to scratch in the little plot of ground Barney had dug up because the gardening fever had hit him. But they soon showed signs of Spring fever in its most primal form. The cocks began to fight.

Three cocks remained after the disappearance of Little Red and Golden Boy. The biggest of the three, a tall Golden Red, with high upstanding comb, large bright eyes, and long curving tail feather, rushed out between the Golden/Red/Black, throwing his head back, proudly announced that Freedom had come to all. The fight broke out.

The tall Golden/Red scratched his wing, circled one of the hens, and leaped onto her. And the cocky Red/Black saw, dashed toward the mating pair, and knocked the tall cock off. But the frustrated suitor turned on the attacker, and the battle for the right to mate with the hens was on. The smaller cock was aggressive. He pushed the fight with vigor, and the tall cock fought back with equal vigor. But the tall cock was driven into the shelter of the Forsythia bush where he rested for a moment, then renewed the fight.

Time and again, the smaller cock drove him into the bush, and each time he came back with renewed energy. Now the smaller cock pecked viciously at the larger one's bright red comb, and struck the larger one with beak and feet, but the tall cock struck back with beak and feet. Hovering close to the ground, wings outspread, eyes glittering, the little cock struck again and again, driving the bigger Golden/Red under the Forsythia bush, and each time, after taking a breath, the Golden/Red came back to strike at his attacker.

This went on for five minutes. To Barney, watching through the window, it seemed like five hours. Then suddenly the smaller cock weakened, he turned tail, and fled. The larger cock followed him for a short distance, then returned to the hens, and to the Middle Man, the Crowing Onlooker, who had watched the fight with continuous loud announcements at each round of the battle. The smaller Red/Black ran, tail down, across the back yard to the honeysuckle clump. Barney watched as the little fellow peered into the clump of honeysuckle vines, found an entrance, and hid himself from view.

Now both the triumphant cock and his Second were crowing amidst the hens on the edge of the old bean field. And silence fell over the honeysuckle vines where Red/Black hid himself in defeat and shame.

Barney stood at the window, watching. Taffy stood close to him, looking up into his face, her own black eyes eager, as if she were saying to Barney, "You just let me out there. I will send them all under the honeysuckle vines, or flying into the trees. Just let me out."

Max rubbed his face against Barney's ankle. He wanted a piece of the action too, but only to run, back bowed, across in front of the little chickens, and send them into spasms of cackling. "Wait," Barney said. "It's twilight already. Soon it will be dark. Stand here with me in the gloaming. We'll see what happens next."

And what happened next? The defeated Red/Black was seen slinking, close to the ground, toward the hen house where the other chickens were gathering on the roost pole. He stopped, hesitant, waited, then he turned and ran, tentatively toward the open door of the tool shed on the back of the garage. At the doorway he paused, looked in, and slowly entered, alert, frightened, uncertain of himself. But Little Grey Hen was on her accustomed roosting perch on the top of the old piano. Now she sang a little song of welcome to the defeated warrior. Red/Black walked in. Barney could no longer see him, but a few moments later he heard him crowing.

Turning to Taffy and Max, Barney said "Now we have a new champion ... and a Replacement for Little Red and Golden Boy both in one battle."

Far into the night, Barney sat reading Charles Dickens' HARD TIMES. Taffy lay sleeping on the floor near him. Max was stretched on his lap with claws hooked into Barney's pajamas. When he could keep his eyes open no longer, Barney went to bed, slept, but rose early to turn on the coffee pot. And listen for the sounds of Day. Then a red ball of fire appeared on the Eastern horizon. It shone through the leafless branches of the trees in the woods on the far edge of the bean field.

Then came the triumphant call in the hen house as the cock flapped his wings and crowed. Barney listened, and heard the answer to the challenge. The Red/Black cock in the tool shed was answering the one, or the two, in the hen house.

Smiling, Barney walked to the door of the tool shed, opened it and looked in. There, on top of the old piano that nobody ever played any more, were Little Grey Hen and her new mate, the defeated Red/Black cock. He was no longer feeling the pangs of defeat because Little Grey Hen sat beside him, singing her strange little song.

In the late afternoon the warmth of the sun lured Barney out again, and he opened the door to the hen house. All the little chickens, hens and cocks, and the one Big Grey Hen, streamed out. Then the once defeated Red/Black cock came out of the garage, followed by Little Grey Hen. He challenged yesterday's champion again, and they fought under the privet bush. Again they attacked and pecked and beat on each other, until the larger cock had worn the smaller one down. Again Red/Black ran away and this time he found Little Grey Hen. Together they left the field of battle and sought the sanctuary of the garage. Golden Red crowed in victory, and his Second seconded him.

But the twice defeated cock's retirement did not last long. Soon he and Little Grey Hen were back in the sunshine, scratching and pecking, but as far as possible from the flock led by the tall Golden/Red cock.

Tale Twenty Five: Two Feathers For A Lion

"What to give a boy whose other grandparents will give him everything? What can I give him for Christmas? What?"

Barney addressed this question to Taffy who was looking expectantly at him with sparkling black eyes. He turned to Max too. Max bowed up his back, ran sideways, and glared green eyed at Taffy.

Barney was thinking of Leo, his grandson who lived far away near the great city of Chicago. He was thinking of Christmas too, and making plans. The big plan was to see that grandson at Christmas. "What will I give him though?" Barney was wondering out loud because Taffy and Max were there to hear what he was wondering. Three little chickens too. Little Red, Golden Boy and Little Hen. Barney was setting a plastic pan full of scratch feed on the ground for them.

Little Red cackled nervously because of Taffy and Max. Golden Boy sidestepped, with his head cocked to one side. Little Hen showed no fear. Cats and dogs and people? They come and go. Life goes on.

"When Leo was here," Barney mused, "he wanted to catch you birds. I do believe that if he could have got his hands on you, his Thanksgiving Day visit to Grampa would have been a red letter day in his life. Not that it was empty, by any means. But still..."

Little Red and Golden Boy had decided that they were safe from Taffy, and Max had not made a move toward them, so they came strutting to the feed pan, still watching with bright yellow eyes. "What will you send to Leo for Christmas?" Barney asked them. Then it seemed to him that the question had asked itself, or had been inspired by the movements of the two little cocks and their one little hen. "What? What?" Barney insisted.

Both Little Red and Golden Boy, living in exile in the garage, had recovered from the violent attacks by the Red and Golden cocks. They had made a good adjustment to one another. "A friendship based on mutual defeat," Barney observed. "And what will you send to the Lionhearted boy who lives far away? For I will fly to him at Christmas. I will be the Santa on his rooftop, coming down his chimney and filling his stockings. But my sleigh will be an airplane and..." Barney's thoughts trailed off and became indistinct because of the confusion of sleighs and reindeers and airplanes. In fact, it started him thinking about the perils of flight, and he said "What can I take for you on the plane?"

Then his eye caught a flash of color on the ground, for the sunlight was now coming through a crack in the wall of the garage. He took a couple of steps toward that flash of color and picked up a bright red feather. Then turning it in the beam of light, his eye wandered and fell upon another feather, a golden one. Both Little Red and Golden Boy, beaten by the Red and Golden cocks, had lost a long curving tail feather. And Barney now held the two lost feathers in his fingers. Little Red cackled nervously, and Golden Boy threw his head back and crowed in response to the calling of the Red and Golden cocks in the hen house a hundred feet away.

"This is it!" Barney exclaimed. "This ... these two feathers will be your Christmas gift for Leo. I will fly to him and deliver your gift on Christmas Eve."

Barney packed the two feathers – one was red with a black overtone and the other was golden with reddish overtones – placing them carefully on the top of his own shirt in the little carry-on bag. And when he arrived at the airport he was searched because the whole country was nervous about hijackings. When the inspector opened Barney's little bag, the first thing he saw was the two feathers, one red and one golden, lying on top of Barney's shirt. He lifted them out, squinting his eyes and twisting his mouth, and he said "What's this?" The inspector looked at Barney as if he had discovered a really strange flier, maybe even a dangerous one.

"Feathers," Barney said. "Chicken feathers." And when the man twisted and turned the two feathers in his fingers, and continued examining the feathers and studying Barney's face with suspicious eyes, as if he were asking himself if he had seen a picture of Barney on the wall at the Post Office, Barney said "They came from the tails of Little Red and Golden Boy. Those two lost them in a fight with the coalition of Reds and Goldens, the other cocks in the hen yard."

"You meet some real kooks in this business," the inspector said. "But go ahead. I don't reckon you can blow up the airplane with rooster feathers ... wait, take off your shoes and let me see." But when Barney slipped off his shoes, there was nothing in them. On the outside edge of the sole of the left shoe though there was something embarrassing to Barney. He didn't mention it to the inspector. In fact, he hoped the inspector had not noticed, and he was very careful not to get it on his fingers as he slipped the shoe back on his foot. Then he picked up the carry-on bag and said to the inspector "the feathers are a Christmas gift to my grandson. Little Red and Golden Boy sent them to Leo."

The inspector repeated what he had already said about the kooks one encounters on the job of examining the baggage of passengers boarding the airplanes bound for distant cities. Barney walked as rapidly as he could to the waiting area where he would join a long line of people waiting to board the plane.

On the plane he sat down beside a woman who smiled and said "Happy Holidays."

Barney smiled too and said "Merry Christmas." Then he added "Grampa comes bearing gifts for little Leo from Little Red and Golden Boy." The woman raised her eyebrows in a manner to indicate that she did not understand and Barney said "Two feathers for the Lionhearted Boy."

Tale Twenty Six: The Mysterious End Of Little Red Rooster

MAY DAY. The rain came down in torrents. The wind blew in gusts. The air was cold. And the two little chickens, Little Red Rooster and Little Grey Hen, came into the utility room and stood looking all around at this place where Barney lives. Little Grey Hen sang her peculiar little happy song. Little Red Rooster crowed furiously in response to the Golden Cock's crowing in the hen house. Both Little Grey Hen and Little Red Rooster turned sharp eyes onto the concrete floor where patches of chicken scratch feed and sunflower seeds and grains of shelled corn were scattered about.

They had come in wet from the rainstorm, but they were happy; they had found a warm dry place of refuge from the weather. Barney watched them happily. "Stay the night if you want to," Barney said, and thought they might sleep on the table beside the fish tank. But Little Grey Hen and Little Red Rooster did not stay the night in the warm dry utility room of Barney's house, and that is why something tragic happened in the night, or in the late evening before darkness fell. For Barney said "I ought to slip out there and close the door. Then they will have to stay." But Barney did not carry out his good intention. Instead, he went back to his chair and his book, and he took a nap.

Then darkness came on and Barney forgot to check on the Little Chickens. He just assumed that they had gone to their roosting place in the big privet bush where they would be safe from night prowlers.

But Little Red Rooster and Little Grey Hen did not fly up into the thick branches of the privet bush; something happened in the cloudy gloaming between the afternoon shower burst of rain and three o'clock the next morning.

Three o'clock in the morning is what is known as First Cock Crow at Barney's house. For that is when Little Red Rooster always sounds his musical announcement that it is time for Barney to awaken because the new day is coming. This new day was a Sabbath Day and on that morning of the first day of May there was no announcement from the privet bush. Barney awakened anyway though. Perhaps it was the silence, the absence of First Cock Crow that awakened Barney. Anyway, Barney awoke with a strange feeling that something was wrong.

"What's the matter?" Barney asked Max, the yellow Manx cat who was sleeping beside him on the bed. "Why doesn't Little Red Rooster sing his early morning song? Do you suppose that something could be wrong?"

Max yawned, stretched his legs, separated his toes and exposed his claws. He looked into Barney's face, then dropped onto the floor and went to see if his food bowl had sprouted any goodies in the night. Barney got up and turned on the coffee pot. He looked out into the darkness, listened to the silence, worried some about the uncommon silence, and went back to bed.

But Barney could not sleep. He lay on his right side, and then he lay on his left side. Max came back and leaped onto the bed. He made big eyes at Barney, but Barney knew something was wrong somewhere, and he could not sleep, so at four o'clock he got up and drank a cup of coffee, then watched for daylight to come in the Eastern sky. Taffy stirred on her little bed on the floor. She opened black eyes and looked at Barney, yawned and struggled to her feet. Barney said "Good morning Old Girl. Do you want to go outside?" Then he thought "there is something wrong outside, and I can't wait for daylight to find out what it is."

Barney finished off another cup of coffee, picked up his flashlight, and said "You come and go with me, Taffy. We have to see…" What they wanted to see was Little Red Rooster sitting beside Little Grey Hen high in the tangled branches of the privet bush. But when he threw the beam of his flashlight into the upper branches of the privet bush, he could not see the Little Chickens, and he turned a worried countenance on Taffy, and said "something is wrong here, Old Girl. Maybe we had better go and look on top of the old piano in the tool shed before we jump to any conclusion though because of that storm yesterday."

Barney opened the door to the tool shed, and shone the flashlight beam onto the top of the old piano, but there was nothing there. Nothing but a few droppings left there where Little Red Rooster and Little Grey Hen used to sleep.

"Five o'clock!" Barney announced to Taffy and Max. "It will soon be daylight." In fact, there was already a faint glow in the sky beyond the wheat field, but that was not what held Barney's attention. He went all about the place, throwing the flashlight beam into all dark corners, but he could not find the two little chickens, and he became very concerned about them.

Daylight came, as daylight always does, but the Little Chickens did not come to the bird feeder in the back yard under the big maple trees. Barney put fresh scratch feed and sunflower seeds and shelled corn on the feeder. He called and called, but all was silence around him. Little Red Rooster did not crow and Little Grey Hen did not sing her strange little song. Finally, about an hour later, Little Grey Hen appeared. She was wet and sad and lonely, and she tried to sing her little song, but it did not come out right. She pecked at the scratch feed, and picked up a sunflower seed, dropped it and tested a grain of corn, but then she turned away, looking all about over the back yard under the big maple trees. Then she ran to the garage and stood there alone and disconsolate. Barney went over the yard again, looking under bushes and in the shrubbery for Little Red Rooster. After looking up into the privet bush seven times, he came back to announce to Taffy and Max "Not a feather! And did it happen in the night? Or did it happen in the afternoon while I was napping in my chair because Tolstoy's War and Peace had made me drowsy, and my eyes were heavy? Surely nothing got him from the privet bush. Even Little Grey Hen was not in the bush. Something got him before he went to roost. It must have been Old Blackie! He's the culprit who carried Little Red Rooster off several months ago. And now he's done it again!"

Now Little Red Rooster's disappearance posed a double problem for Barney. The disappearance of Little Red Rooster meant a real loss in itself, but it meant Old Blackie was suspect. Old Blackie was Neighbor Jim's dog, and this involved Neighbor Jim. "What to do now?!" Barney sat drinking another cup of coffee. But the coffee did not help much. Little Red Rooster was gone, and Little Grey Hen was deeply disturbed.

All that day Little Grey Hen stayed in the garage, alternately singing and crowing and looking desolate. Late that evening Little Grey Hen flew up onto the shelf where all the oil cans and batteries and tools were, and she walked carefully into the nest there and sat down on the three eggs that Barney had left there in the hope that Little Grey Hen would brood. But she had not gone to the nest to brood; instead, she went there for safety and comfort, and when darkness came Barney lifted her off the nest and carried her in his arms to the hen house and placed her on the edge of the nest there, and slipped away.

Next morning bright and early Barney went to the hen house to see what had happened there. Little Grey Hen had left the nest; she was on the roost pole. When Barney opened the door, she flew down onto the floor, and the Golden Cock, now the sole Cock of the Roost, flew down and approached her aggressively, scratching his wing and indicating his readiness to mate with her. But Little Grey Hen was afraid of him, and she flew up onto the roost pole again, wide eyed with alarm. The cock continued chasing her. She became more alarmed. "I will just have to take the risk of letting her run outside," Barney said to Taffy who was standing with raised ears, watching this display of dominance and of resistance among the small flock of little chickens.

Outside, Little Grey Hen went back to the nest in the garage, clucking and swelling out her feathers, and Barney decided that Mother Nature was at work in her own way again. "But what if the killer who got Little Red Rooster comes back and gets her too?" Little Grey Hen settled onto the three eggs in the garage.

The killer was still on Barney's mind when he decided to interfere again. He lifted Little Grey Hen and her three eggs, placed them in the bucket nest in the hen house, along with four more eggs, and marked the date of the expected hatch. May 26, 2004 "Now we will see what we will see." But next morning he looked into the nest and Little Grey Hen was gone. He could hear her clucking. Finally, he found her sitting in the window. "All right, Old Girl. Have it your way," he conceded defeat, carried Little

Grey Hen and the seven eggs to the nest in the garage. She settled onto her eggs and pecked angrily at Barney's hand when he tried to arrange them for her. "Atta Girl. It's all yours. Go to it." Barney turned back to the house and the coffee pot. "Good work, Mother Nature."

TALE TWENTY SEVEN:
CAIN AND ABEL

Maggie had come to visit Barney because Barney had told her that Little Grey Hen's two biddies were growing so fast she would not recognize them if she waited much longer. Maggie is Barney's special friend, and she is always interested in hearing something new about the Little Chickens and their exciting adventures. She said "I'm eager to see whether they are roosters or pullets."

It was a hot August day when Maggie came, and it seemed that Maggie would soon learn whether the two would be roosters or pullets, for a fight was about to break out between the two. But Maggie patted Taffy on the head and asked Barney "Where is Little Grey Hen with her two biddies? How do they keep cool in this hot August weather?"

Barney started to say that they were in the shade of the privet bush, but at that moment Little Grey Hen came running out into the yard, trailed by the two youngsters. "Just look at them!" Maggie exclaimed. "They have grown so much they are nearly as big as their mother. And look at their red combs. I'll bet anything they are both roosters!"

"We will soon know," Barney said. "They are showing their colors. One is dark. He's black with brown spots, and the other is buff colored. But watch! They are going to fight." The two little birds faced off like fighting cocks, flew at one another, pecked, then backed away.

The feathers on their necks were still ruffled up and their eyes were bright with the fire of battle. "What will you name them, Barney?" Maggie was getting excited. "You have about run out of mythical names with Ajax and Castor and Pollux. You will be like the woman who had a hard pregnancy and an even harder delivery, and she breathed a sigh of relief as she got ready to name the baby boy."

"So what did she call him?"

"Alpha and Omega. Because she said he was her first and he would surely be her last."

"Well, I've decided on Biblical names for these two. Cain and Abel."

"Fits the little fighters to a tee. But you are getting so forgetful in your old age, how are you going to know which is Cain and which is Abel?"

At that moment the two little roosters flew at one another again and Barney said "The survivor will be Cain; the dead one Abel."

TALE TWENTY EIGHT: MOTHER FURY

B arney found the baby banty chick outside the wire fence that surrounded the chicken yard. "Hmmm..." Barney observed. "Now what are you doing out here?"

What the baby banty chick was doing was, to put it plainly, was trying to get back inside, and because he was alone on the outside, he was very upset. Going bananas. The two mother hens inside the pen were upset too and they were going bananas in pairs. The four baby banty chicks who were inside the pen were going bananas in fours. Both mother hens, Fulfilled and Frustrated, were clucking and calling to the chick on the outside. The four chicks on the inside were cheeping in concert, and the baby chick on the outside, was struggling to squeeze through the fine mesh wire to get back inside, but the openings were all too small for his growing body. Or his rapidly growing body had grown too large for him to pass through the openings. So he was struggling and flying against the wire because he saw Barney, and he was frightened.

On the other side of the fence, the two mother hens were upset at the prospect of the loss of the one baby chick who seemed to be about to fall into the clutches of Barney who was bigger than all the baby chicks and both their mothers put together. They were strutting and calling to the baby chick to avoid falling into the hands of this monster who seemed about to get him.

Barney reached for the frantic baby chick. "I wiII just pick you up and put you back in there where you belong, with your mothers and brothers and sisters, and fathers and aunts and uncles..." But when Barney reached for the baby chick, he really went bananas, and his mothers on the other side of the fence went big bananas and his brothers and sisters went a whole bunch of bananas.

The baby chick did not want to be caught by Barney. He wanted to go through the holes in the wire, holes that were too small for him. And finding the holes too small, and pressed by Barney's hands reaching toward him, he flew up onto the sides of the fence where the holes were still too small. He was desperate.

On the other side of the fence the two mother hens were desperate too. They thought Barney was going to eat their baby, and so they flew into the fence on the inside, squawking, fluttering and cursing Barney in mother hen language. This went on for what seemed an eternity to the small frightened chick, and to his unhappy mothers. It even seemed a long time to Barney, but he kept after the fluttering baby chick, laying hands on him, and then losing him, and laying hands on him again, until at last he had a firm grip on his small quivering body, and then he held him in his grasp and tried to calm him with soft talk. "Now you are going to be all right. I am not going to hurt you. I am just going to..." and Barney began looking for a hole big enough to slip the baby chick back into the pen.

Held in Barney's firm grasp, the tiny chicken, with throbbing heart and frightened eyes, still struggled to be free. And the mother hens, frustrated, flew against the wire, ruffled their feathers and uttered chicken imprecations against

Barney. At last Barney went to the gate, opened it a crack and released the chick, who flew to the ground and ran to his mothers and brothers and sisters, telling them about his hair breadth escape from the monstrous Barney.

The fury of the mother hens was only partly placated by the return of the baby chick. They continued to scold Barney who was now trying to find the place where the baby chick had got out and he thought he had found it. "Right here under the gate," for there was an opening just large enough for a baby chick to squeeze under. "But of course he would not be able to find his way back inside. So I will just have to close up the gap."

While Barney was fitting a board to the bottom of the gate, he was talking to Taffy, who had been watching with great interest all the while. "I have to stop this now because in a couple of days I will be going to see my grandson and these crazy chickens will ... But I didn't mean to tell you that because you will have to stay at the animal hospital while I am gone."

Taffy's eyes told him that she already knew what he was planning to do and she did not like it, but she would not act in an immature manner about it like these crazy chickens. "So go on and celebrate your grandson's second birthday. I will be big about it. I won't throw a fit like these mother hens."

Barney tested the board at the base of the gate. "If it holds..." And he turned to Taffy. "We have our trials, Old Girl, but you and I, we are grown up people, we just have to make some allowances for the little chickens who don't know any better."

TALE TWENTY NINE: THAT DOG IS HENPECKED

Barney opened the door and walked out onto the front porch. Taffy followed at his heels because there might be something exciting outside. Exciting enough to give up the air conditioned interior of the house. Temporarily. "A little fresh air ought to be good for both of us," Barney commented to Taffy. "Just look. The Little Chickens are running about the front yard and searching for emerging cicadas."

Taffy has no interest in the cicadas that come climbing out of the ground, then up onto the nearest tree or the bannister by the steps, wait for the sun to dry and warm their bodies, then fly off to start singing the mating call. But they are fair game for the Little Chickens who catch them before they can become airborne. "Hope they get 'em all!" Barney hates the high pitched sound they make as they prepare to lay their eggs in the branches of the maple trees.

Suddenly the Little Chicken flock was rocked by an explosion. Little Grey Hen, mother of the two biddies, now called Cain and Abel because Barney found them fighting because they have already discovered that they are roosters, Little Grey Hen, as I was about to tell you, flew up into the air, turned in flight, and landed on the porch. All of her feathers were extended to make her appear twice her real size. Her eyes were full of rage and her rage was directed at Taffy who was standing and gazing innocently out over the surrounding fields of beans, corn, and tobacco.

Little Grey Hen's attack got her attention, for with beak and claws and wildly flapping wings she attacked Taffy violently. Caught by surprise, Taffy yelped and fled to a safer position between Barney's legs. From this place of refuge, she looked up into Barney's face as if to say "Now what have I done to deserve this?"

The assault ended as quickly as it had begun. Little Grey Hen, satisfied that she had established the security of her biddies, Cain and Abel, flew back down to the ground, clucked to her babies, and ran off toward the added protection of the big privet bush. But not quickly enough. For Taffy, indignant over the affair, jumped off the porch, and barking aggressively, scattered the whole flock of Little Chickens, and sent them all running for their lives.

Taffy then returned to the porch and looked up into Barney's face. "What was that all about, anyway?"

"Beats me, Old Girl. That's Mother Love, I guess. Cain and Abel are already big enough to fight, and she's still protecting them from imagined dangers. Anyway, you've been hen pecked and flogged!" Taffy turned back and reared up on the storm door, scratching and making enough noise to get Barney's attention. "Let's get back inside," she was saying, "where it's cool ... and safe."

Tale Thirty: Spring Rites Among The Little Chickens

B arney counted the Little Chickens. Twelve. Six cocks and six hens. "Six perfect pairs," he commented to Taffy. But was it perfect? It would be if the rules of monogamy, so widely expressed by the nation's President, were in force in the hen yard.

But those rules had never been accepted among the Little Chickens. If Barney had mentioned them to the Little Chickens, his announcement would have met loud raucous cackling. So Barney did not mention the One Cock, One Hen rule. Instead he watched and waited to see what would happen. And it did. What happened was that every cock wanted to mate with every hen. Not even Little Grey Hen, the matriarch of the flock, was immune to this attempt at takeover. In fact, she became the prime target for all the cocks. But more about that later.

This is the story of New Big Red, who had gone through some transformations since the possum bit his neck. Now, as the ruling rooster, he fully intended to remain the cock of the walk, and he did not intend to share the flock of six hens with any of the young cocks. Fully capable of maintaining his superiority based on seniority, he exercised his rule with spurs which the young cocks had not yet grown, a powerful beak, and the self esteem that comes from being the Boss when the others were still in the eggs.

But now five young cocks have their hormones turned on, and they all want to mate with all the hens, including their mother. And the Old Boy has a problem. Five problems. He can't be everywhere at once.

As long as they are all fastened in the hen house, he can exercise some control because of limited space. But when they are turned loose, and they go in a stream across the back yard, matters get out of hand. Because the young cocks are all trying to mate all over the place, and the Big Boy is running himself ragged, knocking them off before they can complete the coupling. But there are too many of them operating in too many places, and he hasn't the time and energy left over to do any mating on his own.

Frustration works both ways though. The little hens are run ragged by all this coupling, and some of the less aggressive roosters are lacking for mates. And so desperate they attempt what the President does not approve. Little Golden Boy leaped onto the back of Ajax, but found himself unable to achieve his purpose in life, to mate and reproduce, he struggled to stay in place. "He's sure God trying!" Barney commented to Taffy, who showed no interest in these antics. In fact, she seemed to be saying "If that's what it's all about, include me out."

TALE THIRTY ONE: SURVIVORS

B arney looked at the pile of dead chickens on the floor of the hen house. Then he counted the survivors. Three of the young chickens were still alive. The cockerel and two pullets. These seemed to be unhurt, physically. But they were mentally damaged by what had happened in the night of death in the hen house.

The Big Grey Hen had damage to her head. "I don't see how she can live," he said. "And there is the bigger of the two roosters. He has been bitten about the head and neck. Can he recover?"

Discouraged, Barney turned back to the garage where Little Red Rooster and his Little Grey Hen were watching over a brood of six babies. The rooster has spent the night on top of the old piano, the hen in a box on the floor, hovering over her chicks. "I have cooked rice for the babies," Barney commented to Taffy. "They all appear to be happy and healthy, safe and secure under her protective wings. I've closed all entrances to the tool shed. It looks varmint proof."

Burial detail was scheduled for the afternoon. A mass grave and hard digging. The ground was dry and hard. But the edge of the corn field seemed to be the best place. But it was a sad exercise. Barney then put away the shovel and waited. Two nights later the killer struck again. This time he took one of the two big Golden/Red roosters, and the Old Grey Hen. Even more discouraged than ever, Barney went back into the house for coffee, then again to the tool shed to check on the babies. They were gone.

"Now what? Only a snake could have swallowed them without leaving a trace." The only trace was a very upset mother hen, driven to distraction by the loss.

Barney was desolate too. He went looking for the snake but could not find it. He did find a small hole in the wall between the garage and the tool shed, but a search of the garage turned up nothing. He placed a sharp bladed shovel near the door, hoping that he might surprise the killer. Then he went again to check the hen house. He fastened the entrance from the hen yard, looked all about him in the hen house. But a man can't see everything when he is upset. That night the killer came back and struck again, wiping out all but one frightened pullet and the once proud Golden/Red Rooster with the slashed neck. "I'll have to trap him," Barney said. "Let me see what I have that will work."

He tried a large rat trap, a steel trap that is used by trappers for such small animals as mink. At last he went to the farm store and bought a large cage type trap, the kind he had success in the past for catching squirrels, possums and coons. But no luck with this marauder. Baffled but determined, Barney turned to Taffy. "I'll get him one of these nights, and when I do..." He had been baiting the trap with the remains of the chickens the killer had left on the floor. But the varmint seemed to prefer to make fresh kills.

"There are not many more for him to kill. Little Red Rooster, Little Grey Hen, Pullet. They are all roosting in the rafters over the garage now. What will happen next."

Next morning Barney looked out onto the lawn in the back and saw a much disheveled Golden/Red Cock slinking about under the maple trees. Then this almost unrecognizable apparition hid himself from view.

What has happened to this former Cock of the Roost? Like Saddam, he has been forced to flee and hide. His night in the hen house with the killer has left him a changed bird. His spirit of cockiness is gone. "Fear," Barney says. "Yes. He is now afraid for his life." Joseph Campbell, the man who knew so much about mythology, said that only man knows he is going to die. Well, Joe, no disrespect to your learned person, but this little bird not only knows he is going to die, he has come close to it and now he dreads death. The varmint who raided the hen house, attacked him, hit him about the head and neck, cutting his comb, inflicting physical injury, but worse, he has suffered injury to his ego. He is no longer the Cock of the Roost. He is a frightened little bird who hides in the corn field at night, sneaks out into the back yard in the morning, hoping to feed unseen, and he is chased away by the Little Red Rooster whom he used to chase all over the yard.

He will no longer go near the hen house where he was attacked. He will not face off with Little Red Rooster. He does not strut about the yard as he used to do. The first morning after his release from the hen house, he crowed a few times, a strangled attempt to greet the new day. Now he no longer sounds off at all. All day long he hides in the corn field, except when hunger drives him out of concealment. And at night he sleeps under cover of the tall corn. "Now what will become of him?" Barney asks. "Will the varmint find him one night in the corn field and finish him off? Does his silence cast a light of understanding on the silence of the two little cocks, the first Little Red and Golden Boy, who were caught and carried off by Jim's old black dog, then escaped into the woods? Are they too hiding in silence, their cocky spirits broken?

"And another mystery. Why can't I catch that varmint in my traps? Why do I never see the snake? I am in a killing mood. Yes. I've got killing on my mind."

Barney settled down on the front porch to read. Little Red Rooster and Little Grey Hen came, trailed by Pullet, and there is a difference in them too. They no longer roost on top of the old piano. Is it because they know the killer can climb up there and catch them? "I have found, too late, where the killer comes into the hen house. There is no way I can keep him from getting inside the garage. But look here. The damaged rooster is coming out to the feeder, asking the Little Red Rooster if it is all right for him to eat. Little Red Rooster crows and the bigger bird does not dare answer. The dethroned king is not getting any response from Little Grey Hen and Pullet either. They show no concern for his suffering; it is a sad decline. The vanquished fellow is an object for pity but the other chickens do not even pity him. He has fallen. But they will tolerate him. They will let him stand under the privet bush with them in the daytime but he does not dare enter the garage where they sleep. And not even a strangled croak out of him. He has been accepted on terms of submission, but that is all."

Coffee cup in hand, Barney walked to the window and looked out into the back yard. The sun was shining. Dew was glistening on the grass. Golden/Red was standing out near the Forsythia bush, lonesome, lost, afraid. "He must have spent the night in that bush," Barney said to Taffy. "But how long will he last out there? The night prowler will be back. And how long will Little Red Rooster last on the deck lid of the old car? I am desolate. What is to be done Old Girl?" Taffy yips. "You still have me … and Max. What are you crying about?"

Two more days later: The Fallen Giant is desperate for a place to sleep. A safe place. A roost where he cannot be reached. He has been with the flock of three led by Little Red Rooster all day, but as night draws near he is anxiously trying to find a high perch, and he has selected a big maple tree in the front yard. But an attempt to fly up onto a branch of the tree results in failure. He has lost too many feathers in his encounter with the nocturnal killer. He has also lost some of his strength. Pullet shows him it is easy to fly up onto the branch of the tree, but he has lost his nerve along with his feathers, and he is now running helter skelter in search of a safe place to sleep. He stays close to Little Red Rooster, but Little Red Rooster is no help to him.

At last he has made up his mind. He leaps onto the hood of Barney's old Chrysler under the tree. From there onto the roof of the car and then a flying leap carries him onto a low hanging limb of the maple. Then, walking, climbing higher and higher. Taffy is excitedly barking at him. "What does this crazy chicken think he is doing?"

But Barney is pleased with what he has seen. "That crazy chicken is thinking. That's exactly what he is doing. And he is going to survive because he has learned to think, to plan ahead to a safe place for the night. High in the tree." Barney squinted up into the tree. Couldn't see him at first. Then, "There he is. Safe for the night. Nothing can get him there. I hope."

Now Barney went to check on the three in the garage. Little Red Rooster crouched on the rear deck lid of the old car. Little Grey Hen and Pullet out of sight up in the rafters. Taffy yipped. "Safe?" Barney said. "Safe, I hope. Good night all."

TALE THIRTY TWO: AFTER THE FALL

After the Fallen Prince's thinking apparatus kicked in, it began to appear to Barney that this badly bruised chicken might survive. But with the night prowler still on the prowl, this could not be a certainty. Not even a likelihood. The second night of his thinking phase, the bruised rooster got up into the maple tree, and there he made it safely through another night. But on the third night, Barney moved the car at the very time when the chicken needed it to boost himself up into the tree.

This gave rise to some anxiety on Barney's part, and here is how it happened. Barney's friends, Ken and Jan, met him at the restaurant for dinner, and they sat talking too long about chickens when Barney should have been doing something about that scared and anxious chicken. So when they got back to the house the Fallen Prince was nowhere to be seen. Not in the tree because he could not get up there without the car to boost him. Not in the privet bush where Barney searched with flashlight in hand. Not on the trunk lid of the old car. Even Little Red Rooster was not in his place on the antique car. And Little Grey Hen and Pullet were invisible as well.

"And I wanted to show them to you," Barney said to Ken and Jan. "All three and a half of them. Unless that bad critter has already got them." The critter had not got them. Next morning at daylight Little Red Rooster was crowing on a rafter in the garage, Little Grey Hen was flying up into the Maple tree to show that it could be done without the car for a launching pad. Max had given her the incentive to do it; he was crouching, watching. Pullet was God Knows Where. But when she did show up, the Fallen Prince was with her. That is, he was as close to her as Little Red Rooster would permit. They all ate together though at the feeder, then they all went off to the garage to rest.

"What a relief." Barney passed his hand over his face. "When I saw all those feathers on the ground here earlier, I thought the varmint had got that chicken. And I still don't know where they all slept." He had climbed onto a step ladder, and searched the loft over the garage with a flashlight, and could not see one of them.

In mid afternoon Barney found all four – that is, three and a half – of the chickens under the privet bush. The Fallen One had found a perch about three feet off the ground. Whether this was a safeguard against attack by the Little Red Rooster, or just a delayed reaction to his run in with the night prowler, Barney could not say. "But there they are. And I'll leave the car under the Maple tree tonight, and I'll see if he returns to that perch." Taffy and Max showed their lack of interest in the sleeping habits of the chickens by sleeping soundly through Barney's speech.

In the late afternoon all three and a half chickens were at the feeder. "Little Red Rooster is letting that scroungy looking fellow eat with them, and it now appears that he may even share one of his females with him – the Pullet, when she grows up." The Scroungy Fellow's neck wounds seemed to be healing. The cut on his head and comb had healed over. But he had lost a lot of feathers and will have to grow a new suit of clothing for the winter. Provided he escapes the killer that long. Barney is moving the cage trap into the garage, and will bait it with fresh meat, just in case the killer comes looking and sniffing around again.

August 7, 2003 "I got him. I got the killer." Barney's trapping efforts had resulted in a catch.

He had gone at daybreak to examine the traps, and he had found the culprit inside the cage trap. "A possum!" Barney exclaimed to Taffy who was standing with ears pricked up, eyes sparkling. "Just look." The possum opened its mouth, baring long rows of shining, sharp teeth. Its snout was long and pointed. Its beady little eyes stared back at Barney. "You've taken the bait then and now you are caught." Barney lifted the trap. He set it on top of the bird feeder post. He drew back the hammer on his hand gun. Sent a .38 calibre bullet through the animal's head. "That's your pay for the chickens."

After the shooting, Little Red Rooster crowed triumphantly. Little Grey Hen came running to the feeder, clucking and singing. Pullet joined her quietly "Don't know yet where they slept, but there they are. Still alive. My little family … But where is the Fallen Giant? I don't see him. Did another nocturnal visitor get him? Is he still hiding in the corn? Did this Old possum get him before he went into my trap? … Golden Red, I'm waiting for you to show up, even in your ragged condition."

That Fallen Angel showed up about noon. He came to eat and drink. Then after a brief visit with the flock, he disappeared again. Little Grey Hen and Pullet flew up into the Maple tree in the front yard, looking for a safe place for the night. Little Red Rooster was standing in front of the garage door. He seemed to be trying to make up his mind. Is it safe? Or had I better look out some place where I've never been before? Have I left a scent the night time killer can follow? Barney tried to read the minds of these little fellows and he found it a difficult thing to do, but one thing came through loud and clear: I am afraid.

TALE THIRTY THREE:
WAY UP THERE

The Western sky was aglow with the rays of the setting sun. Beyond the big bean field, beyond the big trees on the edge of the bean field, beyond Barney's ability to see what lay beyond, the evening sun still shed its beams, signalling to Little Grey Hen that it was time. Time for Little Grey Hen to act on the decision that all four of the surviving chickens had made. Barney stood on the front porch, watching. He turned to Taffy, who lay on the cool concrete floor. "Will she make it?"

Taffy made no response. She was not interested. The doings of little chickens did not interest Taffy at the moment. It had been a long hot day. A nap before dark was her prescription for happiness. Barney looked down at Max who was rubbing against his ankle. "Will she make it, Max?" But Max was far more concerned about establishing his claim to Barney's ankle. He might take some interest in that grey squirrel if he ventured closer, but … And Taffy might even chase the grey squirrel back up the maple tree, if she awakened in time to see him, but … Little Grey Hen would have to make her own decision.

Little Grey Hen was busily, anxiously making that decision. Not whether, but how? For the decision to take to the trees had been made when the four survivors talked about it. When they told one another about the attacks in the hen house and when Little Grey Hen recounted the tragedy of the snake in the tool shed. Yes, that decision had been taken, and the Fallen Cock, being the one who had suffered the most damage in the hen house, had already flown up into the maple tree. He was balancing on a limb that overhung Barney's old faded maroon Chrysler. And Pullet had lifted like a bird to take her place up there too.

Now Little Grey Hen ran back and forth under the maple trees. She cocked her head to one side. Her comb glowed fiery red in the rays of the setting sun. Her eyes searched the branches of the tree overhead. She was measuring the distance. Now she crouched, tensed her little body, seemed ready to take flight. Then turned and ran to what might be a better launching site. Again she crouched, her eyes fixed on the low hanging limb. She carefully measured the distance.

Up above, the Fallen Cock, that Golden Hero reduced to fear and trembling by the attack of the possum, peered down at Little Grey Hen. Pullet, the youngest and the most agile of the four, swung back and forth on a small branch until she had gained her balance, then began climbing, one foot after the other, to a higher perch. She settled down about thirty feet above the ground. "She's safe," Barney said to Taffy and Max who still showed no interest; then he turned back to watch Little Grey Hen.

The grey squirrel came nearer. He was picking up grains of corn where Barney had thrown them on the ground under the maple tree. Little Grey Hen showed no interest in the grey squirrel. He was no threat to her. Squirrels don't eat chickens. Squirrels eat corn and nuts and chicken feed, but not chickens. Ignoring the grey squirrel, Little Grey Hen reached her decision. She had raced back and forth long enough. The time had come for action. The measurements were all made, the goal had been selected, the internal organs were prepared. She crouched, leaped, spread her wings, and fluttered upward, and she was there.

Barney settled down onto the top step, opened his book, and began reading. Taffy still lay supine on the concrete floor. Max crouched under the Chrysler.

He was watching the grey squirrel, wondering whether to attack him. He decided against it. That thing could bite and scratch and give him a hard time, unless ... But there was no "unless" with Taffy. She opened her eyes, saw the grey squirrel, leaped off the porch, and made a dash for the grey squirrel. But the grey squirrel was young and quick, while Taffy was old, and even her dash was well ... a bit slow for a dash. The grey squirrel made it easily to the trunk of the maple tree and ran quickly up to safety. Taffy barked to let him know that he was lucky to make his escape, and to let Barney know that she had tried.

Max retreated to a safe place under the Chrysler where he could watch all sides. Taffy's dash for the squirrel had reminded Max of Jim's old black dog who just might show up at any time. But Old Blackie was too big to run under the car. Max would be safe underneath the car, and if Old Blackie tried to squeeze under, Max could break for the maple tree and be up among the chickens while Old Blackie was wondering what had happened to him, so Max was safe and Taffy had performed her duty well, and Little Grey Hen was now up there with Pullet and the Fallen One. But where was the Little Red Rooster, the mate who had once been carried off by Old Blackie, rescued by Barney, and restored to his place on the old piano? Little Red Rooster was having his own problem, and Barney had forgotten him while he watched Little Grey Hen in her flight into the high place in the maple tree.

The Little Red Rooster had watched, from a distance, while the others flew up into the maple tree, but he did not follow them. He ran, instead, to the garage. He leaped onto the deck lid of the antique Plymouth, then flew onto the cross piece in the loft over the car, moved to an even higher perch on top of the plastic cooler, then settled down quietly for the night. All was quiet at Barney's.

The sun disappeared behind the tall trees on the western edge of the bean field. The glow died in the sky. Darkness was coming on. Barney could no longer see to read. "Come on, you two," he called to Taffy and Max. "It's time to go in." Taffy came willingly, gladly. Max had to be caught, and he played the game until he was tired of the game, and Barney was just plain tired. Then he lay down, rolled over, and waited for Barney to pick him up and carry him inside, where he leaped onto Barney's desk and dared Taffy to try to follow him.

So the night passed, as nights have passed from the beginning of time, and the morning came, as morning has always followed the night, but morning did not catch Little Red Rooster sleeping. Instead, a little while before the sun's first rays appeared in the Eastern sky, Little Red Rooster crowed triumphantly from his safe place in the garage loft. The Fallen angel acknowledged Little Red Rooster's rule with silence, dropping quietly to the ground. Little Grey Hen came down too, and began to sing her peculiar song as she checked the ground under the trees for early bugs and other insects. Pullet dropped to the ground too and the Fallen Hero scratched his wing to let her know of his interest in her. "The Fallen One has risen again," Barney exclaimed. "Two miracles. One has risen again, and Pullet has become a hen."

The three who had spent the night in the tree ran toward the feeder in the back yard, where Little Red Rooster waited. One glance from him let the Fallen One know he was still fallen. They all went to work on the scratch feed and Barney said "I'd better get busy and varmint proof the hen house. Who knows how long this roosting in the tree and the garage loft will last?"

Tale Thirty Four:
Just Look At Me

L ittle Red Rooster was running frantically about under the big maple trees in the front yard. He looked up into the trees, seemed about to leap into flight. Decided against it. Not yet. But longing for the heights.

Little Grey Hen and Pullet were already up there on a high limb of the tree in the center of the group. That Fallen Hero had gone up too. He crouched on a limb far out, almost overhanging the road. He had made it by using the old Chrysler as a launching pad, but Little Grey Hen and Pullet had lifted with ease onto the lower branches, then moved on higher. But Little Red Rooster was all alone on the ground.

Until now, he had slept in the garage, in the area above the antique car, hidden from sight. All alone. Now, for some reason hidden from Barney, he did not want to go to his accustomed place in the loft of the garage. Had some night prowler threatened him there? Or was it just the flocking instinct? The need to be with the other chickens? Just to be there with them? Even if it meant a flight into the maple trees where he had never been before. In any case, sitting alone in the garage had become a thing of the past. No more of it.

Now, for ten minutes or more, Little Red Rooster ran back and forth, looking up. He crouched for the leap, seemed to be going to do it. Then he backed out. Never before had he tried to fly up into the trees. Anxiously, he measured the distance against his own strength. And his fear? Then he leaped onto the deck of the old faded maroon Chrysler; he flapped his wings wildly. He crowed. "I did it! Made the first leap." He looked up into the tree again. Leaped again, landed on the car's roof. Flapped his wings wildly again. Crowed proudly. And looked up again. Gathering strength and courage, he became airborne and made it to a low hanging limb, grasped it with his toes, teetered back and forth. Held on. Flapped his wings more wildly than ever. Crowed more victoriously than ever. "Hey. Look at me. I made it!" Never before was a little cock more proud of himself than Little Red Rooster was now. Then came the fall.

For he tried now to move to another branch that looked better, to him. He misjudged the distance. His feet slipped. Or he was hesitant at the last moment. Anyway, he tumbled ignominiously to the ground. Disgrace. Shame. What now? He looked all about him. He looked toward the porch where Barney's friend Joe was watching. He looked at Taffy who was ignoring him. He looked about for Max who was crouching under the car. Then he turned and fled toward the back yard. Toward the garage where a solid area in the loft over the antique car awaited him. But in a moment he came running again to the front yard. He would not admit defeat. Fallen? Yes. Defeated? No.

Now he remembered exactly how it was done, and he followed the known route to the heights again. Onto the deck lid. Flap wings. Crow. Onto the roof. Flap wings. Crow again! Onto the low limb of the maple tree. Flap wings triumphantly. Crow victoriously!

The conquest of fear had come with his first ascent. The victory over shame had come with the second. Now he settled down to sleep. Up there, where nothing could touch him. Up there with the other little chickens. Up there where he could look down on Barney and Joe and Taffy and Max. Up there.

Oh, glorious ascent. Oh proud victory. Oh wonderful flight to the heights.

As the first sign of the dawning of a new day streaked the Eastern sky, Little Red Rooster stood on his limb of the giant maple tree. He flapped his wings, threw his head back, and greeted the world with his announcement that he was its undoubted monarch. Little Grey Hen and Pullet flew down to the ground. The Fallen Angel flew down to the ground. Little Red Rooster remained on his tree limb, crowing. And when he thought he had crowed enough to bring the sun up he too flew down to the ground. Then all four Little Chickens ran to the back yard where Barney had spread scratch feed on a board.

Barney poured a cup of coffee. He turned on the stove under his oats. He looked in his clothes closet for a clean shirt to wear to church. The sun was rising steadily into the sky. But not drawn by the winged horses of the gods. Lifted, instead, by the loud triumphant, incessant crowing of Little Red Rooster.

"All praise to Him Who made the sun and the earth and all creatures great and small, and this herald of the dawn to sing a song that never grows stale but welcomes each new day with joy and hope."

TALE THIRTY FIVE:
SMART IN A STORM

The winds and rains of Autumn brought the leaves showering down. They lay like gold coins, large ones of course, on the ground. Red, yellow, orange, striped and plain brown. The leaves carpeted the ground under the maple trees. As they dried, the wind carried the leaves fluttering, turning and rolling onto the lawn. This remarkable event took place throughout the country wherever trees stood on lawns. But when it happened on Barney's lawn, it caused the Little Chickens to get their heads together again and find a new place to sleep at night.

They cocked their heads to one side, looked up into the bare branches of the maple trees, and said "the wind has blown our cover. Where do we go now?" And they hied themselves to the shelter of the garage where they perched on the fish fin fender of the antique Plymouth. But for only one night ... For when Barney spread feed sacks on the fender to protect it from their droppings, the Little Chickens were insulted and went back up into the trees. Besides, the weather had turned unseasonably warm – Indian Summer? – and the heights were inviting. There they sat silhouetted against a waxing moon.

Next morning though, Little Red Rooster greeted the sunrise with urgent calls from the heights of the maple tree. Then all four of the Little Chickens came fluttering down, and on the ground they put their heads together and traipsed off to the hen house where they found scratch feed and a pan of water waiting for them. This was a very convenient move for Barney. He was planning to visit Grandson Leo at his home near Chicago to go Trick or Treating with him at Halloween and Barney closed the hen house door and the Little Chickens were housed for the duration.

Returning home three days later, Barney opened the door to the hen house; the four Little Chickens dashed out, picked at invisible titbits in the grass, then went back up into the bare branches of the maple tree. But only for one night; next night they just disappeared.

"Where are they?" Barney asked. Flashlight in hand and followed by Taffy, he went in search of the roosting chickens, but he could not find them. "Well, they are hidden from me. I hope the varmints that prowl at night can't find them either." He gave it up, read until nearly midnight, but exhausted from travel, he fell asleep and dreamed badly until he was awakened by the first cock crow.

Little Red Rooster's song put an end to Barney's bad dream about 'possums and 'coons and weasels. The song was coming from the privet bush. Barney breathed a sigh of relief. The privet bush is not what you may think it is. Not a little shrub at the corner of the house. No. It is a clump of thick, heavy foliage, growing on a large group of privet bushes and reaching a height of more than twenty feet and covering a large space that is completely shaded by it for a distance of twenty feet. The branches are all intertwined, forming a little jungle and an effective barrier between Barney's kitchen window and his neighbor across the corn field. "It's a jungle up there," Barney said. "I can hear him but I can't see him."

And from this clump of privet bush Little Red Rooster was greeting the dawn. Then, having settled the matter of the coming of a new day, Little Red Rooster came down, leading his little flock of Little Chickens. On the ground, they faced a wet dawn and they all ran off to the garage to wait and see what the day would bring. Or what Barney would bring to them.

"So there they are," Barney said, speaking over his shoulder to Taffy who had followed him out to the garage. "And very little food for them there. Now we will see how long it takes for them to make up their minds to go back to the hen house." Taffy yipped expectantly and seemed about to run at the Little Chickens, but a frown on Barney's face warned her not to do it.

The Little Chickens did not go back to the hen house. It was a rainy, chilly day and the Little Chickens hovered in the garage for most of the day. In mid afternoon they ventured outside and ran for cover under the privet bush. Barney was watching to see what they would do about the night when his friend Joe came to visit and talk. Even as they talked though, Barney's mind was on the Little Chickens. Joe prepared to leave and Barney said "Wonder where they will stay tonight."

"There they go now," Joe said. "Up into the tree."

But it was only the Fallen One going up. He ascended carefully from limb to limb until he reached the one where four of them had been accustomed to roosting. Then he looked all about, settled onto the limb, and looked down to see if the others would follow. They didn't.

"First one up, but maybe the only one up." Barney watched as the lonely and anxious cock on the tree limb looked down from his high perch. "They are not following the once proud leader. He's lost his place and he sits alone in the tree." Joe nodded his assent, got into his pickup truck, and drove away. Still the Fallen One sat nervously on his perch high in the Maple Tree.

But when Joe had driven away Barney went looking for the other Little Chickens. He looked in the hen house; they were not there. He looked in the garage. Not there either. He checked out the Forsythia but no chickens there either. All of this searching took time, and it was getting dark. What would happen with the one lone rooster in the tree? And where were the other three? Now he went to search in the thick, tangled branches of the privet bush. And there they were. All four lined up, high in the mass of branches and leaves on the bush. About ten feet off the ground. And with the Fallen One nestled as closely as he could manage it beside Pullet.

Yes, the Fallen One had given up his attempt to lure the others to the Maple Tree. Had it been a bid to regain leadership? If so, he had failed, and had to come and seek the company of his companions, and accept again the leadership of Little Red Rooster.

"So chalk up another victory for Little Red Rooster." Barney turned to Taffy with a grin on his face, which she in turn reflected with a yip of happiness. "Little Red Rooster is still calling the shots. It's a rainy, chilly night, but the Little Chickens are together in the privet bush. And with such dense cover, they won't get wet much."

But Barney is a worrier. He justifies this by saying to Taffy and Max "Just think of all the bad things that haven't happened because I worried them away. After two nights in the privet bush the Little Chickens were once more lured into the hen house with scratch feed and water as bait, and when he found them eating, drinking and making merry, he closed the door and tried to ignore the feeling that he had tricked the Little Chickens out of their liberty.

Tale Thirty Six: Singing
In The Rain

B arney was staring through the window at the Little
Chickens running across the back yard toward the
big privet bush. "I will just fasten them up in the hen
house. The weather is too cold and rainy for those Little
Chickens to be out there running around like that." He
looked down at Taffy who was standing by him, looking
up into his face with limpid black eyes that seemed to ask
the question: Will it work?

November in Kentucky is a time for both rain and wind,
and Barney thought: Now how will I get them in the hen
house? So he put the feed in the hen house and picked
up what was on the back yard. The Little Chickens got
hungry and they found the feed. Barney looked in at them
and he said to Taffy "They seem to be content in the hen
house with plenty of food and water." So he closed the
door. Why not?

Well, maybe because that was not what the Little Chickens
would have chosen for themselves. Maybe a bit of drizzle
and blustery cold north wind that turns over the birds'
watering station, and blows over the old thermometer
that's always twenty degrees off on the low side, just maybe
these minor weather disturbances don't bother the Little

Chickens as much as they do Barney. At any rate, Barney noticed the silence on the next morning after he fastened them in the hen house. Daylight came and he heard no crowing from the snug hen house. He said "I'd better check on them. Maybe a varmint has got them." He hurried out into the cold drizzle, opened the door and looked in. No. They were safe. They were standing in the straw on the floor, looking as if they had no interest in what was going on in the world. And Little Red Rooster was silent.

"They're safe. But something's wrong here." Barney looked into Taffy's eyes. Taffy gazed back at him. Max came running and humping to the door of the hen house, as if to say "Let me in there and I'll see what's going on with those silent chickens. I'll stir up some interest and activity. Some noise too."

For two more days, Barney endured the silence, but on the third day he threw open the door of the hen house, the four Little Chickens rushed out bright eyed and excited, they dashed across the back yard to the cover of the privet bush. And there they stayed until in the late afternoon they flew up into the tangled branches and slept there through the chilly, drizzly night. At dawn the voice of Little Red Rooster penetrated the consciousness of a sleepy headed Barney; he raised his head from the pillow, moved his body under the covers, disturbing Max who was sleeping on his feet, and called out to Taffy on her little bed of quilts under the window. "Do you hear that?" And they all went outside to listen to Little Red Rooster's Song of the Dawn, coming from the high branches of the privet bush.

The Little Chickens fluttered down to the ground, they dashed across the back yard, stopping long enough to discover that the feeding pan was missing, then, led by Little Grey Hen, they trailed into the open door of the hen house, ate their fill of cracked scratch feed, and ran out again.

They ran through the drizzle of rain and the blustery wind to a shelter they had chosen for themselves. Soon Little Red Rooster's song was coming loud and clear from the garage where they had found both shelter from the drizzle and freedom to run out through the large crack under the garage door. "So I guess that tells me something," Barney said to Taffy and Max.

"Yes, but what does it tell you?" Max made a dash for the propped open door that leads from the utility room to the freedom of the wide expanses of the back yard surrounded by a hundred acres of winter wheat growing lush and green.

"I believe it tells me that only the free can sing."

TALE THIRTY SEVEN:
WIFE SWAPPING

B arney looked out the window into the bright glow of the rising sun and exclaimed "It's Spring!" Max came humping across the kitchen floor, and Taffy's bright black eyes stared up into Barney's face. "It's Spring!" he repeated. "The grass is green. The daffodils are blooming. The air is moist and bracing. And the roosters are ... wait a minute. That's not Little Red Rooster's voice."

"That crowing," he said to Taffy and Max. Now he listened again intently. Again the sound. Crowing. It was coming from the hen house all right but was different. "Not Little Red," Barney repeated. Neither Taffy nor Max seemed to be disturbed about this new thing. Barney threw open the storm door, rushed out toward the hen house. The sound came again just as he jerked the door open. There the Golden Cock, standing there with chest thrust out, head thrown back, throat expanded, crowing as if the sunrise depended on him.

"Glory be!" Barney said, but then he became concerned. "What's this Golden rooster doing? And what about Little Red Rooster? He's the one who does the crowing around here ... where is he?" But Little Red Rooster was nowhere to be seen. Barney called to him but he did not answer. The

Golden Cock ran past him into the yard. The Yellow Pullet ran out into the yard. Little Grey Hen, walked demurely by and ran after the other two. But where was Little Red Rooster? Barney searched the nests and the corners, and at last he found him, hiding under the metal feeder.

Little Red Rooster crept out from under the feeder. His comb was bloody, his feathers ruffled; fear was in his eyes. Barney knew what had happened. "He's beaten and scared. Golden Cock has risen again to be the cock of this roost." Little Red Rooster now ran past Barney's legs and across the yard toward the house, but he did not go near the other chickens. He ran off and stayed clear of the Golden Cock and the two hens.

Barney turned and announced to Taffy "There's been a fight and Little Red Rooster is beaten." Taffy yipped to let Barney know that if there was a fight she would go in and settle it once for all. "That Golden Cock has not raised his voice since the possum nearly killed him last Summer. Now he is crowing like a triumphant Caesar come home from Gaul. And he has taken over the flock." The flock consisted of two hens, but Golden Cock had both of them. "And Little Red Rooster. What's to become of him now? Poor little fellow. Spring has come. The hormones have kicked in. Mating is on. And he has lost out."

Looking around at the changed situation, Barney noticed Little Grey Hen. She was following Golden Cock as if she had belonged to him all along. "Just look at that little hussy," Barney said to Taffy. "No loyalty. No faithfulness. The two cocks fight and she runs off with the victor. And Little Red Rooster is alone now. What am I going to do about this?"

Almost any reasonable person would have said "I am not going to do anything about this. The Law of Nature has settled it. They fought. The bigger cock won. It is settled.

Leave it alone." But not Barney. He could not leave it alone. He was not almost any reasonable person. He was the man who loved all four of the chickens and especially Little Red Rooster. Had he not rescued Little Red Rooster from the jaws of death when Jim's old black dog carried him off? Had he not gone in a rainstorm and found him hiding in Jim's barn, among all the junk there, brought him home again and set him beside Little Grey Hen on the old piano in the tool shed? So he was not going to let it alone. He was going to do something about it. But what?

"I am going to interfere with Nature," Barney announced to Taffy. Taffy looked back at Barney with question marks in her eyeballs. But Barney had decided to fight Nature. "I am not going to let the Golden Cock have both hens while Little Red Rooster has none." Barney brooded all day on the matter while Little Red Rooster stood off alone and ran about desperately calling for the Little Grey Hen to come back to him. Late that evening he went to his old roosting place on top of the old piano in the tool shed, and Golden Cock led the two hens into the hen house and they all flew onto the roost pole, Golden Cock sitting between the two hens. And when dark came Barney acted upon his resolution to defy Nature and he changed the equation which Nature had set up.

He slipped into the darkened hen house, shone his flashlight beam into the eyes of Little Grey Hen, and lifted her off the roost pole where she was sitting beside the Golden Cock. He cradled her in his arms and walked back to the tool shed. Opening the door, he walked in and set Little Grey Hen on top of the old piano beside the Little Red Rooster. "Now there is where you belong," he said, "with your rightful mate. We are not going to allow any wife stealing here."

Next morning, Barney went to test his experiment, to see if he had straightened out the matter of who belongs to whom. He found out but what he found did not make him happy; for when he let the Golden Cock and the Yellow Pullet out of the hen house, and Little Red Rooster and Little Grey Hen came down from the old piano, Little Grey Hen ran to the Golden Cock, leaving Little Red Rooster sad and forlorn ... Barney was left frustrated. He said to Taffy "The Golden Cock has taken Little Grey Hen away from the Little Red Rooster and my attempt to restore law and order has not worked; it has failed."

But Barney was not willing to give up. He said that maybe one night was not enough to break the hold that Golden Cock had on Little Grey Hen. So when the three returned to the roost pole for the night, Barney fastened the door, and next morning he let Little Grey Hen run free but he left the others fastened up. "Now we will see," he said. "This time it will be a week, not a day."

So it was for a week this time. Little Grey Hen ran about the yard singing her happy little song, in company with Little Red Rooster. But after a week, he released Golden Cock into the yard; Little Grey Hen ran to him and Nature had won out over Barney again.

But Little Grey Hen resisted his efforts to mate with her, and even seemed to be inclined to stay with Little Red Rooster. This led to a renewal of the fight between the two roosters. They squared off, lowered their heads, raised their ruffs, and flew at one another with beak and claw. And it seemed that the Little Red Rooster was winning, even though he had not yet learned to use his spurs which would have given him a real advantage. There was something wrong though. As Barney watched the two cocks fighting, he watched Little Grey Hen too. She went and stood with Yellow Pullet and seemed to Barney to take no interest in the fight and to have no bet on its outcome. And yet there was something...

Suddenly Little Red Rooster gave it up and ran away. Little Grey Hen immediately went back with the Golden Cock, and he strode away with both hens. "Faithless strumpet!" Barney exclaimed. "Is this the real reason for Little Red Rooster's fall? Is it that he recognized the fact that his faithless wife has deserted him for the larger, flashier Golden Cock? And what am I learning about these Little Chickens now? Are they so much like us people that we fail to see ourselves in them?"

Night was coming on, and Barney went searching for the Little Chickens. He found the Golden Cock and the Little Grey Hen sitting high in the privet bush. The Little Red Rooster crouched on top of the old piano in the tool shed. "But where is the Yellow Pullet?" he asked Taffy who followed him every step he took. "Well, one more place to look." He looked inside the hen house. Yellow Pullet sat alone on the roost pole.

"So. Here is another revelation. She is saying that if the Golden Cock has taken up with that Little Grey Hussy, she will not have anything to do with them. She will just roost alone ... and in here."

Then Barney had another idea about all these goings on. He picked up Little Red Rooster, lifting him gently from the top of the old piano, and carried him to the hen house. There he set him down beside Yellow Pullet who took alarm at this intrusion and flew down onto the floor. But Barney beat a hasty retreat from this scene and closed the door. "Now it's up to you to achieve such connubial bliss as you are capable of. I am going to my own bed. I have done my deed for this day." He slept with clear conscience and even though he knew he had pulled a trick that might backfire.

Long before daybreak, in fact, at first cock crow, he was awakened by the song from the privet bush, and another from the chicken house. "Might as well get up and see what will happen when daylight reveals my deed," he said to Max who was already prowling.

Daylight came. Barney poured his second cup of coffee and stood at the window, looking out toward the hen house, and what he saw made him chuckle so that he spilled some of the coffee on his foot. There was the Golden Cock running frantically about the chicken house and pen, searching for the Yellow Pullet. "Oho!" Barney laughed. "Now he is really in a swivet. Well, I'll just let him sweat it."

Barney finished his coffee and went out to the chicken pen. "Now we will just play another trick," he said, opening the gate to the chicken pen. The Golden Cock rushed inside and began calling to Yellow Pullet to come and join him, but she could not come to him because the door between pen and hen house was closed. The Golden Cock was now more frustrated than ever. He could neither get to Yellow Pullet nor return to Little Grey Hen. When he had enjoyed Golden Cock's frustration enough, Barney opened the door and let the Yellow Pullet run out to join her anxious lover who immediately began trying to show her some wonderful grains of corn he had found on the ground in the pen. Then Barney released Little Red Rooster into the back yard where he and Little Grey Hen were united after a fashion.

Grinning broadly, Barney went back to the house, poured himself another cup of coffee, and stood at the window, watching Little Red Rooster and Little Grey Hen feeding together under the maple trees. He turned to Taffy and said "I wonder if he will forgive her now. Serve her right if he makes her stand on one leg to do penance for her sin."

On this second day of April, in the year two thousand and four, with frost on the lawn and bright sun rising beyond the wheat field, the Little Grey Hen droops about in the garage. She seems forlorn and unhappy, even though the Little Red Rooster stands close beside her, crowing loudly and proudly in a bellicose manner, in answer to and as a challenge to the Golden Cock in the hen house.

Is she lovelorn for the Golden Cock? Is she refusing her rightful mate, and overcome by some strange mating force beyond the ken of Barney, a mere human? "Have I done wrong then?" Barney asks himself. He sat down in his reading chair. Max leaped onto his knees. Taffy cast a mournful eye at him. "No help from you two. Neither one of us speaks chicken language."

Barney has now become thoughtful. "Do I have the right to meddle in the mating instincts and practices of these Little Chickens? I have been critical of the President's attempt to meddle in the mating habits of people. Am I now doing the same thing here in the chicken yard? And am I playing havoc by doing it? Is this why neither Little Grey Hen nor Yellow Pullet will brood? What to do?"

So next morning Barney let the Golden Cock and the Yellow Pullet run out into the yard and the contest broke out again, for when Yellow Pullet ran toward the maple trees, Little Red Rooster chased her and mounted her with great gusto. But the Golden Cock saw and he ran and knocked Little Red Rooster off.

TALE THIRTY EIGHT: YOUR OWN MOTHER!!

Little Grey Hen is the matriarch of the hen yard. Any act that violates her position is a serious matter that requires severe punishment. If not in the normal pecking order of the hens, then the punishment must come from that cock once called Golden Boy who fought Little Red for supremacy, and was then attacked by the 'possum and reduced to fearful subserviency, and then rose again to be the Supreme Ruler whose reign has not yet been challenged. Since there is none Bigger or Redder than he, we will now call him the New Big Red, for the one who was once Big Red, a Rhode Island Red, was traded off because he had become a tyrant whose free wheeling could not longer be tolerated in the flock of Little Chickens.

So. New Big Red. But now there is also a Young Red. He is the son of Little Red, now sadly deceased but not forgotten, and Little Grey Hen, the Matriarch of the whole flock. This Young Red is as tall as New Big Red. He has long curving tail feathers. Touches of green among the red and black feathers on wings and body. But no spurs. For he is yet a young fellow.

But his hormones have kicked in, and he is crowing, strutting, and scratching his wing as he circles the pullets.

He tries to mount the pullets who are themselves reaching maturity with bright red combs to indicate their readiness. They are even laying an occasional egg. So Young Red is in competition with New Big Red for mating rights with the females of the flock.

These pullets, less colorful than the cockerels, are shy and timid. Clothed in dull browns, light yellows and buffs, they try to avoid Young Red's courting advances, and this is frustrating to Young Red, for when his hormones kicked in, they kicked in powerfully. So he is looking about the hen yard, and whom does he see with a red comb? None other than Little Grey Hen herself.

Yes, Little Grey Hen has mothered that one yellow chick long enough. We do not know whether to call that chick Twelfth or Dozenth, but she has decided that chick is big enough to look after himself/herself, and she has other things to do. She is laying eggs again; her comb is fiery red; and she is noticeable to the cocks. To both the New Big Red, and the Young Red. And this is cause for trouble. For Young Red, rebuffed by the pullets, and assuming that the New Big Red is busy some place other than the immediate environs of his amorous intentions, attempts to mount Little Grey Hen. And he is almost successful, but not quite. For while he is struggling to attain his balance on Little Grey Hen's back, the New Big Red sees what is going on, and he dashes to the scene, flashing anger; he attacks, knocking Young Red off, and driving him ignominiously from the hen yard. Young Red flees into the hen house; in hot pursuit, New Big Red follows and gives him a sound thrashing there. Barney, listening to the angry sounds coming from the hen house, hears "And your own mother!!!" What Young Red's sounds mean may be left to the reader who will see him emerge from the hen house, thoroughly chastened, but not convinced that he had done wrong, only that he had been caught trying.

Castor and Pollux – they are the twin sons of New Big Red and Pullet are standing by, watching, alarmed, and wondering if they will be the next target of their father's wrath. These two are handsome young cocks, golden with brown and blue and green in their wing feathers, with long curving tail feathers; so black they glisten in the sun. Brown specks on their breasts. Where the tail feathers sprout from their backs, the white underclothing shows, they hold their heads high in their pride and wonder. So far, they seem safe, for New Big Red knows they are his own, and that Young Red is Little Red's son, so he is partial. But these two, so much alike that even Barney cannot tell them apart, are getting ideas too, and they are eyeing the pullets.

"Soon we will see," Barney remarks to Taffy, who stands watching the spectacle. "Soon we will see what the New Big Red will tolerate from his own sons, the handsome Castor and Pollux.

TALE THIRTY NINE: THE HATCH AND DEATH

On this fifteenth day of Little Grey Hen's brooding on the seven eggs, she came off the nest, dusted herself while her mate, the Little Red Rooster, looked on proudly, then ran shakily about the front yard, attracting attention to her unusual condition.

She looks like a ghost hen," Barney remarked to Taffy. "Just imagine that. Fifteen days on that nest, warming those eggs, without any rest. No wonder she has pushed one of them out and never even noticed it."

Yes, that is what Little Grey Hen had done. And that one egg was a mystery to Barney. There it lay in the feed pan outside the nest, and Barney wondered if another hen had dropped it there. Wondering, he cracked it open and found an almost fully formed chick inside. But dead.

Now the little mother-to-be was having her first holiday, and she was eager to be near Barney where he was sitting on the steps with his ever present book. She hopped up onto the porch, but Taffy, always the watchful watch dog, drove her off. Then, as though she had just remembered, she dashed off to the garage, fluffing her feathers and quarreling "like an old setting hen" and took her place again on the nest, covering her six eggs.

"All right Old Girl," Barney laughed, "six more days and we will see what you can do. I am guessing that Mother Nature has already programmed you for the job. Six more days, and you will have the job done. Well, the first part of it. The Creation."

On the twentieth day of July, 2003, Sunday morning dawned both sunny and muggy and four brown and yellow chicks emerged from their eggs under the Little Grey Hen. Barney found the Quadruplets lively and already exploring their new world. Two eggs remained at eight A.M., and Barney's midwifery duties were carrying over into church time. He waited, watching, expectant, but a bit concerned about those two eggs.

"I'll give Little Grey Hen more time," he commented to Taffy. "These four seem to be a day early, by my calendar. Just wait. We will see."

The proud father, Little Red Rooster, started crowing before dawn and he kept it up until the four babies had hopped out of the nest and into a pan of cracked grain. Only when Barney came to remove the maternity operation into a cardboard box on the floor, did Little Red Rooster leave his perch on top of the old piano, and run outside for a bite of breakfast.

"You've done a fine job, Old Boy," Barn told him. "Go now and take it easy. I'll leave those bigger roosters fastened up for a while so that they can't rain on your victory parade. Yes, you've done yourself proud. Bravo."

Little Grey Hen is proud too. She dutifully pecks Barney's hand every time he reaches in to examine the babies, and to check the two remaining eggs. The Quadruplets are lively. One has already hopped up onto his mother's back and begun to ruffle her feathers with his little beak. All of them are pecking at the food Barney placed in the box with them.

"Everybody's proud as punch," Barney declared. "I wonder if I ought to mention it at church this morning ... Well silently to the Lord, maybe. And maybe just a whisper to Bill and Betty."

Barney returned from church to find Chick Number Five newly hatched and still wet. Little Grey Hen was fussier than ever, and Barney lifted her off the brood, set her on the floor, and she promptly jumped back into the box.

One egg remains.

Barney went to fix his lunch while Chick Number Five dried off. Quintuplets now.

During the night Chick Number Six broke through his shell.

But during that same night, death struck in the hen house. A killer came and wiped out the flock, killing six, maiming two, and leaving three scared out of their wits. He had eaten part of one of those killed. Now only the Little Red Rooster, his mate the Little Grey Hen, and their six babies remained untouched by the tragedy. What happened in the hen house while Barney slept, and even Taffy, the Watch Dog slept on the floor by Barney's bed, and Max, the Night Prowling Cat, sat perched on the back of Barney's chair? Who was the killer?

"I cannot understand it," Barney declared. "Yesterday, my friend Joe, watching the little chickens streaming across the lawn, asked What will you do with too many chickens? Today I am asking What will I do with too many dead chickens?" Barney continued his reflections. "Yesterday I was looking proudly on a thriving flock of beautiful birds; today I am viewing a scene of devastation and desolation. And preparing for burial. Life and death in one terrible night.

"How did the killer get in? I thought I had varmint proofed the hen house and the pen with fine mesh wire. But there was an opening somewhere. And I had grown lax. Obviously, the killer slipped through the wire, then through the open door from the pen into the house. He did his killing job and walked away.

"But why did I hear nothing? They were a noisy little flock. Setting up a racket of cackling at the least disturbance. Why did they not awaken me? Did they die in silence in the darkness while they would rouse the dead in daylight? Will I ever know? And will I know the killer? I will try to trap him and make him pay for the death of my Little Chickens."

Barney examined the remaining birds. Three of the young ones, the cockerel and two pullets. These seem to be unhurt, physically, but mentally damaged by the trauma of that terrible night of death. The Big Grey Hen has so much damage to her head that it is doubtful whether she can recover. The bigger of the two roosters has damage to head and body. Will he recover? If he does, it is unlikely that he can be the cock of the roost again. Little Red Rooster is now the only hope. He has fathered a brood of six new chicks; he stays at night on the old piano, watching over his wife and children. Barney has cooked rice for the babies. They eat hungrily and seek the protection of Little Grey Hen's hovering wings.

Brian and Joe, friends of Barney, came to help with the burial. It was a mass grave in hard, dry ground at the edge of the corn field. And great sadness as the once proud and the beautiful were laid to rest beyond the reach of the killer.

Tale Forty: How The Grinch Almost Stole Christmas

B arney opened the door to the hen house and looked on the scene of devastation. Dead chickens were lying all over the floor. Feathers scattered everywhere. The survivors standing mute and terrified on the roosting pole. "What in hell!" Barney exclaimed. "Some varmint has got in and killed my Little Chickens!"

There had been twelve. He had named that one lone buff chick Twelfth. Now there were six. Six living. Six dead. Four cocks two hens left after that night of death. He gathered up the dead and buried them in the edge of the wheat field. Threw the door open. Turned the living loose in the yard. "Leave this death house. I have to make it varmint proof before you can come back in."

Outside, the six Little Chickens went about in fear. Evening came. They flew up into the trees to roost. Counting, Barney saw only five. "A hawk?" He searched the yard and found a bunch of feathers. Next morning, when they came down, there were four. "An owl?" Or had the varmint climbed the tree?

Next evening the four went into the privet bush, but when the morning came, there were only three. Barney was desolate.

Two days passed. Two nights. Then morning, and when Barney took the coffee can of sunflower seeds to the garage, he called, listened, saw and heard nothing. He called again, waited. Then heard a single cock crow. He lifted his face. The single cock was standing on top of the old car. He threw out his chest, threw back his head, crowed again. "There you are! Still alive. Christmas is almost here. Can you make it?" The Little Cock crowed again. "Let the Grinch be damned!"

Tale Forty One: The Sad Ending Of A Happy Tale

Barney's three year adventure with the Little Chickens had been one of great satisfaction with intermittent tragedies. He had come to recognize in them the human traits that made them most companionable and, at the same time, indicative of those human traits that are most endearing and sometimes disturbing. But as all good things seem destined to end, the adventure with the Little Chickens ended in tragedy. Death struck in the hen house one night in late summer or early fall. When Barney opened the door he faced both death and the forecast of more death. Six of the Little Chickens lay dead on the floor, their bodies mangled, half eaten. Feathers still floated in the air. The six living, some of them injured, stood terrified on the roosting pole. When he flung the door wide, the survivors fled the house of death, ran into the yard, never again to enter the place of their terrible night.

Barney stood, watching the six Little Chickens run toward the protection of the privet bush. He was both angry and desolate. He gathered the dead, and prepared to bury them, wondering aloud. "What could have done this? I thought we had made the place varmint proof. And maybe it was big varmint proof. But a mink? A weasel? Even rats?

There's not a crack big enough for a coon or a 'possum. Could it be a skunk?"

He carried the dead and mangled carcasses to the edge of the wheat field, brought the shovel from the tool shed, and began the sad job of burying his beloved Little Chickens.

All day the six frightened Little Chickens hovered under the maple trees in the backyard, occasionally seeking the protective shadows of the privet bush. Early in the evening, they began actively seeking a safe place to sleep. They flew up into the maple trees, testing out the places on the limbs. Five of them settled for the more dense branches of the privet. One little hen settled onto a branch of the maple, about twenty feet high. Barney watched anxiously, talking again to himself. "Maybe they'll be safe up there. But when morning came the little hen had disappeared from the high branch of the maple tree. Had an owl come on silent wings and with extended talons, and carried her away?" As good a guess as any." Barney scattered food on the ground for the five who came down from the privet bush.

For two days the five Little Chickens ran hurriedly about the yard, hiding at times under the privet bush, coming out to eat and drink. "Maybe if they keep to the privet bush at night..." But on the third day the two remaining hens were taken. "In broad daylight!" Barney exclaimed. "A fox? Coyote? Old Blackie, my neighbor's dog?" They had disappeared without leaving a feather.

One week until Christmas. Three roosters. One of them was missing his tail feathers. But they came quietly when he called them to come for their sunflower seeds in the garage. First one of them crowed. Then the other two. "Trying to be brave," Barney said, congratulating them. "Will we make it until Christmas?"

Two days later only one Little Rooster appeared for the morning ritual. Barney looked at him closely. "Yes. You are Cain. I said you would be the survivor. You have the mark on you." As Barney waited for Christmas, Cain heralded each morning from his perch in the privet bush. And when he went to feed him. Cain came and sang his morning song to him. Christmas came, Cain was still there. Even though Barney went away for three days to spend Christmas with his family at Chicago he left the feed pan full, and when he returned, there was Cain.

"If you make it through the winter, then I will get a little hen to be a mate for you in the spring, and we will start all over again. But three weeks into the New Year, Barney awakened to the silence. There was no sound from the privet bush. He went and called but Cain did not appear under the maple trees in the back yard. He searched the garage and the tool shed. No Cain. No new droppings on the roof of the old car. Only quietness as the sun rose without the herald to call out its rising.

"It is the end." Barney turned back to the house. "An owl has come in the moonlit night and taken my brave Little Fellow away."

An After Word

I t has now been a long, lonely time since that last brave little cock was taken by some night prowler, and some changes have come to the small area which was the kingdom of the Little Chickens.

Taffy has gone, the victim of old age, to be replaced by Spirit, her mirror image, and Spirit was drawn by her curiosity to the edge of the highway where she met her death. Now Sheba, a black and white Border Collie, does the barking here, and fills the empty places left by Taffy and Spirit. But Sheba knows nothing of the Little Chickens.

Only Max remains with memories which erupt at times; then he makes a bow of his back, and dances sidewise to let me know ... what? Maybe he is just letting me know. The question is, what do I know now that I didn't know before I brought the Little Chickens home from Trade Day at Mayfield, and they filled the place with both beauty and joy ... and sadness?

I have been thinking about our world at war and writing about what is happening in our world at war, and making some comparisons with the little flock of Little Chickens running about the yard here, a microcosm of the larger scene, a little world of both ambition and conflict on a minor scale, small enough to be seen all at once, except when one strayed away and caused me to wonder where the wanderer had gone. And I have reached some conclusions.

My conclusions are about human nature, and I have reached these conclusions by watching and experiencing at first hand the loves and the fights and the struggles and the hopes of the Little Chickens.

The Little Chickens who lived under my constant gaze were just like people in their social order. Or, to put it the other way around, people are just like the little flock of Little Chickens in their attempt to form and perpetuate a social order.

It is a matter of establishing dominance and maintaining control over the occupants of the territory. Big Red must be the Cock of the Roost, and he will be until his dominance becomes overbearing, and he has to be removed and replaced; then Little Red becomes the dominant factor until a coalition of the ones being dominated puts him down and takes control.

This results in a division of powers. The ousted ones form a harmonious relationship, even a friendship of the defeated.

But there is also a force from outside, a threat from above or down under, a predator more deadly than the forces contesting the crown. This force destroys both the conqueror and the beaten in the now divided flock. Eventually this force will kill and consume them all.

While all of this is going on, another force, the mother force, is producing new life, ever hopeful and protective, and given the opportunity, would save the community. But when the outside force is too great ... and the individual members of the flock are incapable of forming a collective force to oppose the destructive outside force, the members of the flock will be picked off one by one until the last one is gone.

How sad and lonely God must be, as he looks at what is happening to His world! His Beautiful Little Mythic World, spinning among the million shining heavenly bodies. Spinning into death and darkness.

Little Chicken Tales   Henry A. Buchanan

Epilogue To Little
Chicken Tales

Now I look back on my three years experience with the Little Chickens. I am overwhelmed with sadness. For I loved them and now I have lost them. I fought a losing battle to keep them, and they fought more valiantly than I did to survive the attacks made on them by varmints of the night, birds of prey, and the neighbor's dog. They were happy little birds when they ran free on the lawn under the big maple trees. They were cocky little fighters as they competed for the right to mate and perpetuate themselves.

They were devoted little mothers who were willing to fight for their babies. They were joyous proclaimers of the coming day, and they dreaded the night because the night held threats too great for them. And they gave me great joy and happiness, but their loss has left a sadness that lingers for years after they have gone. So I have shared their story, my story, our story, with you in the belief that in knowing the Little Chickens you will know yourself better and gain a greater respect for the least of God's creatures.

Yes, I could have built a modern chicken house, varmint proof, to take the place of the old ramshackle barn. I could have caged them or penned them in an enclosure that no predator could penetrate. But they would not have been happy because they would not have been free. And I would not have had the joy they gave me when they ran free, chasing, fighting, and exulting in their freedom.

Goodbye, Little Chickens, I loved you. And I believe you loved me. Goodbye, Little Grey Hen. You will always be on my shoulder - in my memory. And I will always hear your strange little song - in my heart.

Henry A. Buchanan
19 October 2009

ABOUT THE AUTHOR

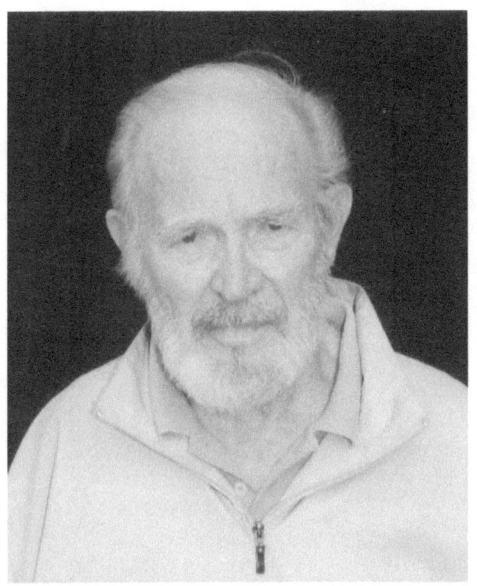

Henry Buchanan was born and bred on a Georgia farm with little chickens running about his feet. He lives now in rural Calloway County near the little university town of Murray, Kentucky. Surrounded by corn and bean fields, he kept and cared for the Little Chickens he writes about with humor and pathos and an understanding that brings these winged bipeds together with four legged animals and people in an inspiring anthropomorphism that leaves the reader wondering who is talking to whom the most.

Author of twenty-one books ranging from "And the Goat Cried" to "The Shellman Story: Hanging the Preacher", Buchanan brings these "Little Chicken Tales" out of his own experience.